Dr. Julian Hosp

CRYPTOCURRENCIES

simply explained

Cryptocurrencies simply explained
Copyright © 2019 by Dr. Julian Hosp

ISBN-13: 9789881485083

ACKNOWLEDGEMENTS

This book would not have been possible without the support of quite a number of people helping me with proofreading, feedback, and ideas that propelled this book to life.

I am especially indebted to all those fantastic discussions with various people from the crypto-ecosystem that allowed me to widen my knowledge and all the people on social media asking questions and challenging me constantly to provide better, simpler knowledge.

Further, I would love to thank my family, whose love is with me in whatever I pursue. I am especially grateful for my dad, who instilled a high curiosity for technologies at an early age—without it, I may have never had that detailed look at the cryptographic field in the first place.

As with my previous books, I am entirely grateful for Patricia Zinnecker, who is always there to assist me with any matters that might come up. But most of all, I want to thank my fiancée, Bettina, who always has my back and motivates me when I need it most.

And last but not least, I want to thank all who have helped me along the way, although I am not mentioning them directly. I am truly grateful to each and every one of you.

Dedicated to my father Laurin Hosp,
as he started my technical curiosity.

TABLE OF CONTENTS

ACKNOWLEDGEMENTS

This book would not have been possible without the support of quite a number of peoplle helping me with proofreading, feedback, and ideas that propelled this book to life.

I am especially indebted to all those fantastic discussions with various people from the crypto-ecosystem that allowed me to widen my knowledge and all the people on social media asking questions and challenging me constantly to provide better, simpler knowledge.

Further, I would love to thank my family, whose love is with me in whatever I pursue. I am especially grateful for my dad, who instilled a high curiosity for technologies at an early age - without it, I may have never hat that detailed look at the cryptographic field in the first place.

As with my previous books, I am entirely grateful for Patricia Zinnecker, who is always there to assist me with any matters that might come up. But most of all, I want to thank my wife, Bettina, who always has my back and motivates me when I need it most.

And last but not least, I want to thank all who have helped me along the way, although I am not mentioning them directly. I am truly grateful to each and every one of you.

FOREWORD
BY DR. HARALD MAHRER

The dream of a better world has moved humanity since the dawn of time. At the instigation of the famous humanist Erasmus of Rotterdam, the English statesman Thomas More published his work Utopia in 1516. This document, which describes an „ideal society", is today regarded as one of the most important forerunners of social utopian conceptions, often dealing with the equitable distribution of goods and simultaneously with the abolition of money. Following highly dynamic technological developments today - 500 years later, the prevailing models of society are questioned by different thought leaders with regard to their future sustainability. Individual freedom versus state compulsion and control, or more personal comfort and an easier life for the price of the loss of privacy? All these are metaphors for fundamental questions of the digitization of our world and the convergence of man and machine.

For the apologists and masterminds of the crypto-economy, this new form of decentralization of systems is the path towards a possible utopia, a blockchain-based and, as it were, better and more just world. With the present book, Julian Hosp provides insights and outlooks into these potential spaces. It offers the opportunity to understand basic technical functions of the crypto-economy and to recognize its potential. The focus is clearly on getting to know the cryptocurrency subsystem, the first publicly-inclusive expression of the entire crypto-economic ecosystem.

I thank Julian Hosp for his work and this book and I hope that by building up knowledge and personal reflection, the readers actively participate in a necessary debate about the dark and light sides of a crypto-economic development. So far, the question remains unanswered how ecologically sustainable or supported by market-economic principles a blockchain-based world can contribute to a prosperity-promoting competition. On the contrary, there are more questions than answers and more paths to the future than we can imagine. Therefore, in sticking with the credo of the Enlightenment, we need to have the courage to use our own intellect. Sapere aude! And this book makes an important contribution to this.

Dr. Harald Mahrer
Federal Minister of Science, Research and Economy
Republic of Austria

WHAT TO EXPECT

Have you ever asked yourself what a cryptocurrency, a blockchain, or Bitcoin is? How about the word "decentralization?" You might have heard that "these things are coming" and "will take over the world." No matter if you have or haven't, "they" are right—these things are coming. And "these things" will play just as important a role as the internet has for the past 20 years.

You know who "won" with the internet? The people who started preparing for it at the beginning, using it personally or for their business before others did. Maybe you were one of those early adopters or maybe you missed the first wave, but you certainly know of people who caught it and are now ahead of the curve, either because they made a lot of money through investing or by making some smart business decisions in that regard. With this new technology called blockchain, a similar window of opportunity has started to open.

If you have no clue what a blockchain, a cryptocurrency, or Bitcoin is, don't worry—most of the population doesn't. If you do, however, would you know how to explain these things in less than a minute to a 10-year-old? Chances are that your answer is "no." I know this because I give close to a hundred talks a year all around the world on this topic. "No" is most always the answer, no matter whether it is in Europe, Asia, America, or Africa. Even when I enter a room full of blockchain developers and I ask who could explain a blockchain, but then add "in under a minute and to a 10-year-old," almost no one raises their hand. Looking at these facts, one starts to wonder how the general public should ever understand these breakthrough concepts so they hit the mass market.

One of the main challenges for anyone trying to get familiar with the topics around blockchain, decentralization, Bitcoin, and other cryptocurrencies is the question of "Where should I start?" This is exactly what prompted me to write this book. In the simplest way possible, I will explain all the aforementioned points so even a 10-year-old could understand them. At the same time, I will reference the details on a technical level to give you both the large scale and the detailed picture. Explaining something to a 10-year-old is in no way a commentary on anyone's intelligence. I'm just following Albert Einstein's advice:

"If you can't explain it simply, you don't understand it well enough."

Maybe you can recollect the times you had to explain something to a child (maybe your own). You could not use the same terms and words you would normally use. Initially, this was difficult, but once you figured it out, you gained a totally new understanding yourself. Can you remember an instance like that? Following this principle, I want to explain these new tech terms around blockchain in a language that truly anyone can understand—even a 10-year-old. This will not only help you understand everything better, but furthermore, it will allow you to explain these things to other people if you wanted to. The ultimate goal is to make people all around the world #CRYPTOFIT. I.E fit for this new wave of decentralization and blockchain. Are you open to joining the ride with this single point of entry?

Aside from the simple language and pictures I'm using, I will add some techy-geeky stuff. It's pretty much the same info, just on a more complex level. It will be highlighted as such, so you know when parts come that you could skip if you wanted to, or don't quite fully understand yet. You will not miss out on any info; it's just there for those of you that love numbers, math, and cryptography.

ADVICE

One important thing before we get going: I have created a 20-page printout summary that goes with this book that you should definitely download. The PDF will help you even more in understanding and keeping an overview of the ideas and concepts laid out. You can keep it next to you while going through this book, and it will help you understand certain terms and concepts. Additionally, if new updates come out, I can add them in the booklet for you to have the latest news included. Simply go to www.cryptofit.community/workbook and download it for free!

IMPORTANT

The book is structured in a very specific way, BUT you can jump to any chapter upfront, if that is what interests you most. For example, if you mainly want to learn about investing into cryptocurrencies, jump to that chapter right away. Nevertheless, it is recommended you go through the book in the order it is set up.

WHY LISTEN TO ME

At this point, you might just be reading a teaser of this book, and you don't really know who I am or why you should trust me on this journey. It begs the question: "Why should you actually listen to me?" I get it—what gives me the right to talk about the topic of blockchain, cryptocurrencies, bitcoin, ICOs, and related tech? There are so many people out there spreading info about it, so why should you believe me out of all of them? Fair question. So, let me tell you a little bit about myself and how I got into the cryptocurrency space.

After having studied medicine in Austria for six years, I graduated and started training as a trauma surgeon as part of my residency. I had been one of the Top 10 professional kite surfers in the world for almost ten years leading up to that. Suddenly "being locked" into a hospital for almost 100 hours a week was not the life I had envisioned after having traveled all around the world as an athlete. So, in 2012, I decided not to continue my work as a medical doctor and chose to combine my knowledge of a professional athlete and medical doctor to offer coaching, personal development, and training to others. I moved to Hong Kong to gain some experience in business, finance, and marketing, which all were areas I had very little experience up to that point. I have always preferred actual experience over traditional school education, therefore that move made a lot of sense to me. Trying to set foot in a city between the Western and Eastern worlds were some tough years, but it taught me a lot about rejection, public speaking, and money.

In 2014, I felt that I had enough. So, I decided to quit living in

Hong Kong, and I started to travel again, still working in personal development. Purely coincidentally, I met a fellow Austrian, and his friend from Thailand in Bangkok on a layover. We hit it off straight away, especially on one specific topic: cryptocurrencies. I had heard about Bitcoin in 2011 from a patient of mine, but I hadn't paid much attention to it ever since. Recalling that Bitcoin back in 2011 was valued around 1 USD, it was a shock to hear that it had now gone up to roughly 1,000 USD. My first thought was: "Wow, had I invested 1,000 USD in 2011, I would have made a million dollars in just three years." I had written it off as a scam in 2011, but after our talk, I became really interested in it. After our meeting, I started to research everything I could about blockchain, cryptocurrencies, and bitcoin. It was not easy to understand, but still easier than some of the medical material I had to study in the years prior. The hardest part was figuring out where to start. Whenever people ask me whether I ever regret not working as a doctor after having studied all those years, I answer no. It wasn't time wasted, but rather the foundation for understanding all the tech-stuff in the crypto-world.

Over the following months, we kept discussing various interesting ideas, but most of all, how to bring these virtual currencies to the masses. In May 2015, DBS, one of the biggest banks in Singapore, hosted a blockchain hackathon in Singapore. This was basically a weekend-long event where several teams tried to convince an investment panel of their project's merits. We prepared a pitch to win the 15,000 USD in prize money. You can watch a video from back then and how we got prepared by looking for the YouTube video: "Julian Hosp hackathon Singapore."

We did well and ended up winning. On the side, I started to make a few videos on blockchain and Bitcoin to explain it to the people. But I was not yet fully convinced about the success of these new concepts, especially after Bitcoin had this massive downtrend in 2014 and 2015 after the hack of an exchange called MtGox. If you search for "Julian Hosp Bitcoin and blockchain—this is why you should care," you will find one of my first videos ever and will notice some uncertainties in my explanations.

It was also then that I gained the conviction that these new concepts were here to stay, and I knew that the education of the general public on these topics was essential. So I started a YouTube channel (www.youtube.com/julianhosp), a facebook group (www.facebook.com/groups/cryptofit), and a podcast (http://kryptoshow.libsyn.com); all of them have become some of the largest in the world.

It became my personal mission to help people understand what block-chain and cryptocurrencies are and how they work, so that at least 1 billion people around the world get to know about this topic through me in one way or another by 2025.

I know this sounds like a crazy mission and vision, but this is what I grew truly passionate about. It's how the brand and hashtag "#CRYPTOFIT" was born—to make people fit in cryptocurrency skills. Today, I have guest-authored hundreds of magazine articles on popular blockchain and other fintech opportunities. I have met with regulators, central banks, and top finance people all around the world, and Influencive named me as one of the top crypto-experts to follow in 2017 (https://www.influencive.com/top-blockchain-cryptocurrency-experts-follow-2017/).

So, this is what you will get out of this book that you will not find anywhere else:

- Some "educators" of the crypto ecosystem are actually NOT INSIDE the system. They just report on it from the outside.

There is a huge difference between sources with hands-on knowledge of cryptocurrencies and those just rehashing what they've read. That is why it is very important for me to not only write a book about this topic, but to actually build a successful company that gives me a whole new perspective.

- Some people claim to be blockchain experts to push a hidden agenda onto their followers. The lack of knowledge allows many scams to take advantage of people. I am committed to educating people in the most transparent way. I approach all of this from a different angle. Yes, of course, I would like people to use the products and services of my company, but the main goal is to bring this exciting ecosystem closer to a billion people all around the world.

- Many self-declared "thought leaders" are stuck on a certain topic, not looking outside the box. They get fixated on a specific cryptocurrency or project. This book is about the broader idea of a decentralized system. What this actually means you will find out soon. I don't see myself as a "fanatic" trying to convince you to buy an individual coin or token. I want you to get the hang of the ecosphere as a whole and show you how centralization and decentralization can and will coexist together.

- Early adopters often have a highly technical background. Many times, this leads to explanations being confusing and difficult to understand for beginners. I have more of a scientific background, which allows me to explain complex concepts in simple terms, while still covering the essentials. In my opinion, that is the secret to success: keeping it super simple.

Simplicity

Complexity

So, with all that said, I am glad that you actually got this book into your hands. Once finished, you will be truly #CRYPTOFIT. If you want to read up on some other details about my life, check out my personal website: www.julianhosp.com. If you want to read a book about my life prior to cryptocurrencies, go on Amazon and search for "25 Stories I Would Tell My Younger Self." This book became a bestseller in 2015 as it is an easy read with fun stories and valuable lessons.

For consistent updates, follow me on Social Media—I would love to connect with you there:

www.facebook.com/julianhosp (well you know… Facebook ;-)
www.twitter.com/julianhosp (regular thought snippets)
www.linkedin.com/ln/julianhosp (many professional themed posts)
www.youtube.com/julianhospenglish (lives & weekly videos)
www.instagram.com/julianhosp (personal pictures)
www.julianhosp.com/podcast (Kryptoshow Podcast)

We have three very awesome communities that you should definitely join if you want to be around likeminded people. Remember, proximity is power!

German Facebook Community for Q&A: www.facebook.com/groups/kryptoganzeinfach

English Facebook Community for Q&A: www.facebook.com/groups/cryptofit

---

TIP

Before we get started, have you downloaded the 20-page workbook? You will need that after every chapter to get an even more in-depth understanding of what was covered. Download it here: www.cryptofit.community/workbook

---

Enough about me, let's get started to get you #CRYPTOFIT :-)

CHAPTER 1 – FROM GOLD TO CRYPTO

If you truly want to understand what cryptocurrencies are, we have to start with a brief detour through history to actually conceive what the concept of money is. Don't worry, this will be brief and painless. ;-)

WHAT IS MONEY?

Il denaro potrebbe essere considerato come un insolito tipo di energia. To break down what money is in its most basic form, it's nothing more than any method to transfer some type of value (the product of someone's labor or ingenuity) from one person to the next. Food, salt, animal hides, gold, silver, IOU coupons, and just about anything shiny—each has served as money at one time or another. This value that we call money can then be converted into all kinds of other things, such as services or products.

Obviously, money has changed its shape over the past years: from physical coins and papers to more digital versions. This transformation has been going on since before recorded history. What started off in the year 10,000 BC as the trade of basic survival goods, such as animals, salt, sugar, and so on, turned into the use of precious metals as "money" around 2,000 BC as societies grew ever more complex.

WHAT IS A CURRENCY?

A currency is the actual execution of the theoretical concept of money. For this to work, a currency needs to fulfill three criteria:

1. Be a good **store of value.**
2. Provide an efficient **method of transfer.**
3. Be a good **unit of account**, so you can measure and compare.

Most important, all three attributes need to be **trusted by the community**. This explains why animals, livestock, shells, and many other things are simply not good money. They are not good currencies since they do not store value well; they can be hard to transport and difficult to measure and compare. Of all currencies though, the oldest and most well-known is gold.

GOLD AS MONEY

The oldest known form of money, gold, has a few very important advantages over the use of other goods when we look at the three points that make a great currency:

1. **Gold is rare and cannot be reproduced**. It doesn't just grow on trees. Getting it out of the ground requires work. Using other goods like animals, sugar, or salt does not necessarily fulfill this criterion. **Gold doesn't perish or change and cannot really be consumed.** This is a very important characteristic. Yes, gold can be used for jewelry, but it still stays gold. Thereby, gold seems like a good **store of value.**

2. **Gold is transportable.** Gold has a very high density and takes

up very little space. This is a big advantage over, for example, livestock, and makes gold seem like a good **method of transfer.**

3. **Gold is fungible.** This means one ounce of pure gold is the same as another ounce. There is no ounce more or less valuable. Two half ounces of gold have the same value as one full ounce. This makes trade a lot easier and was one of the main reasons people moved away from shells or precious stones like diamonds, where one is unlike the other. For example, with diamonds, there is the 3 C rule: Cut, Color, Clarity. Based on these three factors, the value of a diamond is defined. So, while two stones might look the same, they might be worth completely different amounts. Gold, on the other hand, seems like a good **unit of account.**

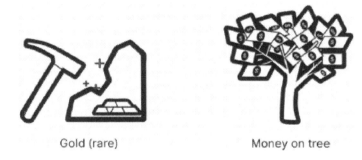

Gold (rare)   Money on tree

Trust is the most important factor for a currency to be seen as money, and gold is definitely trusted. Why is that?

WHAT IS TRUST?

Whenever I ask what kind of "money" people think is the best, most reply with "gold." People do this because they trust gold. They accept a bar of gold because they firmly believe that someone else will accept it from them. Thousands of years of familiarity has only engrained that trust.

> **IMPORTANT**
> There is no inherent value in gold, as you cannot eat, drink, or use it. Gold gets its value through trust based on its history, as it has proven time and time again to be rare, fungible, transportable, and non-perishable.

Understanding the three keys to a currency and how gold beats other forms of currencies is very important for understanding our current paper money—also called fiat money—as well as cryptocurrencies. We have to check all the points, just like we did for gold, to understand why something could or couldn't be used as a currency. The more characteristics we find to check against the three core points, the better.

WHAT ARE IOUS?

Gold was used as the main type of money for over 3,500 years (2,000 BC to 1,500 AD). In the mid-1500s, people began to notice a few disadvantages of using gold as a currency:

1. First of all, fraudsters started mixing gold with other cheaper metals, thereby diluting the actual original value. It had be-

come difficult for the average person to see whether one piece of gold was actually the same as another. Coins became less rare and had thereby become **not such a good store of value** after all.

2. Second, people grew tired of having to carry something extremely heavy with them. They looked for alternatives, as gold was **not such a good method of transfer** after all.

3. Third and lastly, while gold is divisible in theory, actually halving an ounce of gold into two half-ounces is quite the challenge in a typical store. Maybe there was a better possibility, as gold was **not such a good unit of account** after all.

While gold was good enough, people looked for a "better" system. They found it in **paper money pegged to gold**. The concept was simple: You give gold (or silver) to a bank, and they issue a document called an **IOU ("I Owe You")**, which you can then use in the real world just like you had used gold before. Paper money was a lot lighter, it was easy to issue smaller valuations instead of one larger one, and the issuer could make them quite difficult to fake. Let's look at the characteristics of this new currency compared to gold itself to make sure IOUs are actually a good form of money:

1. Store of value? Yes, because every IOU is pegged to gold and that is rare.

2. Method of transfer? Better than gold, as paper is very light.

3. Unit of account? Better than gold, as one paper is like the other, and it is divisible into smaller papers.

Trust: As it is connected to gold, which gets its trust through history, the trust question is sound. After a short initial hesitation, people did see the benefits of this new currency, and paper money became prevalent in society.

WHAT IS FIAT MONEY?

Great, so what is wrong with our paper money today, you might ask? Why do so many people complain that today's money is "bad money"? Well, that's in large part because the "gold-pegged-money" does not exist anymore. This might surprise you because you might believe that your dollar or any other currency is still "backed by gold." Let me drop the truth bomb: After around 450 years, in the 1950s, most countries around the world dropped the so-called "gold standard" by disconnecting their money supply from gold. Even the US Dollar, the world's reserve currency, abandoned the gold standard in favor of "free floating" on the open exchange market in 1971. The driving purpose behind all this was allowing governments to better manage inflation and deflation by controlling how much money was in circulation. Suddenly, any central bank could increase or decrease the money supply at will. Money became a commodity, worth only what people were willing to pay for it in foreign markets, or worth only how much trust the locals had in a currency in the domestic market. This new type of money without any pegging to gold became known as **"fiat money"**.

In this book, I will not use the term "backed by gold," as it leads to the question, "What is gold backed by?" Eventually, we would see that all gold is backed by are the three points of a good currency and how gold had built up trust over history. Since this trust is so ingrained into our minds, we see something backed by gold as the "gold standard," where all we actually need is something that can check those three required bullet points. So, let's look at the points for fiat money—paper money NOT pegged to gold. Matching it up to gold will reveal why so many people have raised concerns over fiat money:

1. Method of transfer? Lighter and easier to transport than gold.
2. Unit of account? Much easier to count and audit than gold.

3. Store of value? Fiat money is only rare for you. You can NOT print new money, but the central authorities now can, since it is NOT pegged to gold anymore, which kept them from multiplying currencies at will. This printing of money is called **inflation** and describes when the money supply is increased and thereby the value of money decreased. Fiat money is NOT a good store of value if the government prints money and inflation eats up its value.

We now have a completely new scenario. Instead of trusting the connection to gold, we have to trust something completely new: a central authority, who we hope will take care of this fiat money and make it a good store of value.

WHAT ARE THE ROLES IN A MONETARY SYSTEM?

For a monetary system to work, three things have to be governed:

1. Access to money
2. Sending and receiving money
3. Supply of money

These three points can either be governed in a centralized or decentralized manner.

WHAT IS CENTRALIZATION?

With fiat money, we have a single organization that holds the power to do whatever they want with this new money. Of course, with great power comes great responsibility. As long as this centralized organization does not misuse their power, all is good...but what if they do? The trust in gold has now shifted to a "centralized trust," where a central organization holds "all the power."

> **IMPORTANT**
> The trust of our fiat money is based on the central authority, where people trust the government or a central bank to make sure our money is "safe."

If you want to summarize what happened in one sentence, you could say: With fiat-money, money became centralized. During the times of gold, it was decentralized.

WHAT IS DECENTRALIZATION?

Decentralization means that everyone who wants to be part of a community or system has the same rights and possibilities. No one is more or less than anyone else. With gold, all financial matters were regulated in a decentralized manner. No one and everyone was in charge. Anyone could go and dig up gold. Anyone was allowed to own it. With fiat money, the central bank of any government is in charge of the financial system.

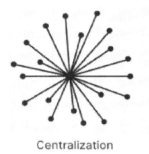

Centralization

Decentralization

Centralization then took another step forward when money became digitized around the new millennium.

WHAT IS THE MAIN CHALLENGE WITH DIGITAL MONEY?

While it is a lot more convenient to exchange numbers on a screen in comparison to trading actual animals or gold, it comes at a huge cost: Multiplying animals or gold to get more money is quite a challenge and requires work and time. Printing more paper money is quite easy if you are the organization in charge, but multiplying digital money on a screen is as simple as adding a few zeros to your account balance.

In order to avoid fraudulent behavior, governments made money more digital and ever-more centralized. Central institutions were put in charge to decide who can open an account, manage transfer limits, and most important, keep the balances of the people in a community. Without that last control, everyone could just copy and multiply money on their computer at will. With gold or physical money, that had not been possible, so there was good reason for a central institution to take over. All around the world, central banks work together with local banks to manage your account balances. They decide:

- When you can access your money (for example, Monday through Friday from 9AM to 5PM)
- How much you pay to access your money (withdrawal and transfer fees)
- How much money you can access at any given time (transfer and withdrawal limits)
- Who can actually access the monetary system (billions of people around the world do not have access to bank accounts or credit cards)
- What your balance is (even in first-world countries, balances can be "garnished" or accounts frozen for a variety of court-mandated reasons)
- What the actual money supply is (inflation, interest rates, etc.)

In most instances, it is absolutely fine that a central institution is in charge, as long as the people trust it and it does not misuse its power. Obviously, digital money has its advantages:

- Storage cost and transport are way lower compared to physical goods.
- If you have a 100-dollar bill, you can't just cut it in half to have two 50s. With digital money, this is just a split on the screen.
- Digital money is a lot faster to process and audit than physical.
- Adding more points of acceptance is easier as the exchange of different currencies can happen on a technical, rather than a physical, level.

MONEY AS A METHOD OF CONTROL

Centralization gives money a new function: Control over the people who want to use it. The central organization is in charge and can dictate what people can and can't do with their own money. Therefore, many people have asked the question of whether it was possible to have a digital (nothing physically needed) monetary system with all its advantages, just without a central party to trust in. Such a system would be:

1. Completely open for anyone to join.
2. Completely without borders or transaction controls.
3. Accessible 24/7.
4. One with clear rules that everyone can see and track.
5. Completely trustless, as all you had to do was to trust the system itself.
6. Very difficult to hack, as no central party had all the money.
7. Even further attack-proof by offering multi-signing abilities, where the signing keys could be put at different locations around the world. There's no single "safe" that someone could break into (like to steal gold), but rather several at the same time.

While this sounds really great in theory, let's compare this to a "gold standard type of money:"

1. Store of value? Problem, because if no one is in charge, what keeps someone from printing new money? The money supply is not governed. Therefore, this digital currency is not rare and a bad store of value. So, it will only be a good store of value if a 1 on a screen will stay a 1 and cannot be altered by

someone at will.

2. Method of transfer? Better than anything physical, as it is digital.

3. Unit of account? Better than anything physical, as it is digital.

What about trust? The major problems of a decentralized digital system are that of governing "money supply," "access," and "receiving and sending." This is why we use central authorities for digital processing today, but if there was a way for those problems to be solved, we would have a near perfect monetary system. For quite some time, people were trying to figure out a way to solve the problem of scarcity in a decentralized digital system, where no one was in charge, per se. In 2008, a very promising idea to this so-called double-spend-problem was proposed, which is what we will talk about in the next chapter.

WORKBOOK

At the end of every chapter, I will list a summary of things you should have learned in the 20-page workbook. If you haven't downloaded it yet, you should do it now, as it will help you understand the content of each chapter even better: www.cryptofit.community/workbook

These are a few examples for this chapter:

What three features make a currency?
What different types of trust do gold, fiat, and cryptocurrencies rely on?
What is centralization?
What is decentralization?

The 20-page workbook is designed to be used along with the book and should be used for notes and as a summary after every chapter. It will help you deepen your understanding while also giving you an excellent overview over the entire topic. www.cryptofit.community/workbook

CHAPTER 2 – BLOCKCHAIN AND CRYPTOCURRENCY BASICS

WHAT IS THE DOUBLE-SPEND-PROBLEM?

The double-spend-problem can be best understood by using the example of a picture on a phone. If I upload it onto Facebook, I just made a copy. This cost me basically nothing. I can then also upload it onto Instagram. Again, pretty much at no cost. I just "double-spent" my picture, but since that does not really affect anyone in a harmful way, no one cares. This is why no one monitors whether I upload it once, twice, or even a hundred times.

Now imagine there is a digital currency called the Julian-Coin. Bob has a hundred Julian-Coins and he sends friend A all hundred. Just like with the picture, Bob clicks copy and paste, and now has an extra hundred Julian-Coins at literally no cost. He now sends these extra hundred Julian-Coins to another friend. He pretty much did the same things as with the picture—only this time, his friends care because money represents a form of value and trust. In a normal financial system, a bank will make sure Bob could not have done that, but if we want to have a decentralized (so NO central institution) monetary solution, we have to find a way to avoid double-spending without having a governing body.

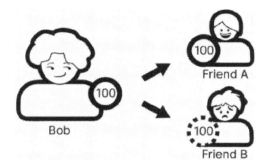

In 2008, an individual or a group (no one really knows) called Satoshi Nakamoto stipulated a solution to this double-spending problem in the 2008 whitepaper, "Bitcoin: A Peer-to-Peer Electronic Cash System" (https://bitcoin.org/bitcoin.pdf). The groundbreaking idea in the 8-page paper is the introduction of a blockchain to remove a central party and still be sure that no one could cheat.

WHAT IS A BLOCKCHAIN?

In short, a blockchain is a decentralized community's complete and unchangeable transaction history that everyone who is part of the community agrees on. This ledger automatically gets updated in regular time frames, is accepted by the community as a fact, and gets stored on every participant's computer. This way, no central party has to govern the community, since no one can double-spend. That would create an immediate conflict in every participant's transaction history.

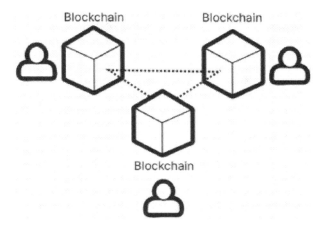

Instead of a central party dictating what is "reality," the community does so in a decentralized manner. Blockchain technology thereby allows storage of any kind of "reality" without needing a governing body. This can be applied to any type of ownership, identification, knowledge, or…currency.

HOW IS A BLOCKCHAIN USED FOR A DIGITAL CURRENCY?

Blockchain technology provides the infrastructure for a digital currency to exist without a central bank. Currency is one of the many different applications that can run on a blockchain, using the benefits of decentralization in the digital world.

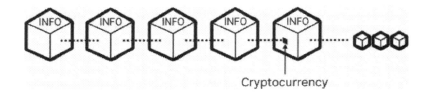

Cryptocurrency

Since this currency on a blockchain uses cryptography, it is called cryptocurrency.

WHAT IS A CRYPTOCURRENCY?

In a cryptocurrency, any rule or regulation is programmed into the cryptographic algorithm that governs the decentralized community using the currency. The combination of cryptography and currencies gives crypto-currencies their name. This basically means a currency that is backed by and made rare through cryptography.

> **IMPORTANT**
> Trust in a cryptocurrency is derived from the underlying cryptography. Since this is a new concept compared to thousands of years of using precious metals, it will take a bit of time until more and more people start to understand the true benefits of the new system.

BLOCKCHAIN AND CRYPTOCURRENCY NOMENCLATURE

To clear up some confusion, let's define a few terms:

Blockchain: the immutable transaction history of a decentralized community.

Cryptocurrency: an application using blockchain technologies by which the transaction history and therefore the exact amount of currency everyone owns gets stored via a blockchain.

Bitcoin (B capital): is used to name the idea and protocol of the first decentralized cryptocurrency on a blockchain.

bitcoin(s)—lower case b: the currency itself.

For example: "Thomas has learned about cryptocurrencies, however, he is more excited about the blockchain, rather than one specific application. Still, in Bitcoin, Thomas owns 12.7 bitcoins, as he believes the value will go up, and he found that investing into the blockchain itself was not possible."

WHAT WAS THE FIRST DECENTRALIZED CURRENCY?

There have been several cultures around the world that refused to have a centralized monetary system. While it is very hard to say which one was the largest or first, the concept of Rai stones on the island of Yap is quite fascinating and describes the concept of a blockchain and decentralized currency in an easy to understand way. The islanders did not own much gold, so in order to have some kind of currency that everyone could have access to if they wanted, they carved huge round stones out of limestone. They would then be used as currency. In theory, every islander would have been able to do this, but it mostly became a specialized task done by a few, while the others preferred to sell products or services to receive such stones in return. The system was decentralized, as it was completely open for anyone to join, and everyone had the same rights.

However, if you look through the criteria for something to be seen as a good currency, there was one huge problem: transportation. It was a nightmare to transport these stones from one place to another. The solution? Instead of actually transporting the stones, the islanders stored the stones at specific places, like in front of a church, house, etc., and then passed along virtual ownership. This worked by the islanders informing everyone else in the community who they had just given one of the Rai stones to. Suddenly, the stones were not only a great store of value and unit of account, but also a good method of transport—without them actually having to be moved from one place to another. It was based on a decentralized system, where every islander knew who owned which specific stone.

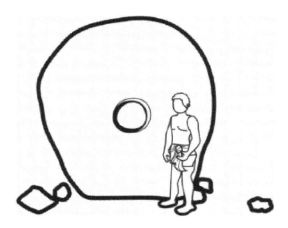

Looking at blockchain and cryptocurrencies, you will soon recognize how similar this concept of the Rai stones actually is—with the difference that Rai stones are physical, and cryptocurrencies are digital. That is why cryptocurrencies need a blockchain as an underlying technology. This distributed ledger avoids a double-spend, since every coin's ownership on the blockchain is traceable by every participant. On Yap, the three tasks of a monetary system (access to money, sending and receiving of money, and supply of money) were decentralized by making the Rai stones difficult to make and eventually easy to transport (via virtual ownership). Cryptocurrencies also need to solve these features, and in the next chapter, we will discuss them step by step.

CHAPTER 3 – PRIVATE KEYS AND PUBLIC ADDRESSES

The first thing we have to solve in a digital monetary system, when we want to send money from one person to another, are accounts.

HOW DOES DECENTRALIZED ACCOUNT MANAGEMENT WORK?

In banking, you have a bank account number so that people can send you money. Your bank account number is unique; there is no one else who has the same number. Otherwise, if you gave someone your account number to transfer you money, someone else would be receiving that money. The same works with e-mails: When you sign up, for example for Gmail, the service checks whether your email address has already been taken to avoid an address conflict. This only works because services like a bank or Gmail are centralized services. As long as they do their job well, everything is good. But what if the bank decides to just close your account, or Gmail doesn't let you access your emails anymore? What if the centralized service misuses its power?

In a decentralized system, this is exactly what cannot happen because there is no central party that owns the database of accounts. It cannot shut you out or take anything from you. But how does it avoid two people in such a system ending up with the same "address?" There are a couple of true breakthroughs in blockchain technologies that most people are not aware of. This address solution is one of the things that truly excites me every time I think about it.

The solution comes through cryptography with a private key and a public address.

WHAT IS A PRIVATE KEY AND A PUBLIC ADDRESS?

Since there is no centralized database when you register, instead of you getting to select an account, you simply receive a random number (called a private key or seed) that is either a string of letters and digits or a set of random words. In the case of Bitcoin, which is the most famous cryptocurrency, you receive a random number out of 2^256 possibilities. That's a number with a 1 followed by 80 zeros:

100.000.000.000.000.000.000.000.000.000.000.000.000.000.000.00
0.000.000.000.000.000.000.000.000.000.000

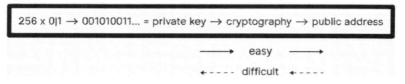

The number of account possibilities is insanely large, around the same amount as there are atoms in the visible universe. Normally, this private key is not displayed as the actual number, but in its hexadecimal form with 64 digits/letters. For example, like this:

E9873D79C6D87DC0FB6A5778633389F4453213303DA61F20BD67FC233AA33262

Instead of generating this private key yourself, most of the people in cryptocurrencies let a computer program generate this private key (password) for them. You need your private key to send money, just like you need an email password to log in to your account and send an email. But now comes an important difference in cryptocurrencies: Instead of you getting to choose the so-called public address, it gets mathematically derived from the private key. Imagine it as if in Gmail all you had to type in was a password because there was an email address automatically assigned to that specific password. The way this works in Bitcoin is through Elliptic Curve Cryptography, and SHA256- and RIPEMD160-functions. If you want to dig deeper into how this works, simply go on Google and search for "Julian Hosp cryptography." I have a lot of videos and blog posts where I get into the nitty gritty of these things.

The important thing about these mathematical functions is that it is literally close to impossible to guess a "password" (private key) if you just know an "e-mail address" (public address), but it is mathematically very simple to get to the public address if you know your private key. As a simplified demonstration, imagine it as if the private key were a random number, and the connected public address was the 2nd power to that. So, if your private key was 8, your public address would be 8-squared or 64. This is something that most of us could still do on a piece of paper ourselves. But let's try the opposite direction. If I told you my public address was 289, what would my private key be? If you didn't have a calculator by hand, the only way to find that out would be through probing: What is the square-root of 289? 15? No, too small. 20? No, too big. Somewhere in the middle—17 it is. Correct. Now, imagine this being done with numbers that have 50 or more digits. It would be easy to square any of these numbers, but it would take quite some time to figure out the reverse.

The example of squaring was just a simplification, as in actual cryptocurrencies, this process is a gazillion times harder. Even if you combined all computers in existence to solve these problems, the universe would come to an end before you could find a solution. There are simply the same number of possibilities out there as there are atoms in the known universe. It is so hard to guess a private key from a public address that it is statistically more likely that you could run towards a wall and all your atoms would start a so-called Quantum Tunneling Effect at the same time, letting you pass through the wall without ever touching it. Ever experienced that yourself or seen someone do that? Nope, me neither, and that's why it is impossible for anyone to guess your private key or for two people to receive the same private key. Again, it is more likely that you could start running through walls without ever touching them than receive a private key by chance that someone else has been using to store Bitcoin before you. If you don't believe me, start trying by running through walls.

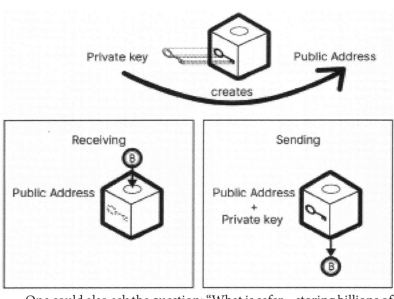

One could also ask the question: "What is safer—storing billions of dollars in a safe where the location is known and all one had to do was break through the security (centralized banking or email version), or having gazillions of completely open safes out there, knowing that in one of them are billions of dollars inside, but it would be taking longer than the universe could exist to check in which safe all the money is in?" It is just not as familiar, and thinking about a random number, that in theory could be the same as someone else's, is not a nice thought, especially when we hear news that some supercomputers have been trying to generate Bitcoin addresses with money in them and succeeding. How is this mathematically possible? It turns out, simply by the original creators of the Bitcoin address not having used a system with a proper random address generator. That's why it is especially important only to use services that are open source and have been tested over time. Not doing that is like using 1234 as your password.

> **TIP**
> In the chapter about wallets, you will learn about great services that do not have this problem and the generation of addresses is truly random.

For those of you that want to understand the actual cryptographic process, here is the geeky nerd-version for Bitcoin, which can be skipped by those not interested in the math details.

A Bitcoin address, for example, starts with a 1 or 3 and could look like

GEEKY

Careful, "Nerd-mode ON"

1. Start with a randomly chosen private key from 1 to 2^256.
2. Use Elliptic Curve Cryptography, where the private key is the "multiplier."
3. This is your public key.
4. Do a "Hash160" by using a SHA256, followed by a RI-PEMD160.
5. Do a Base58Check as a "Checksum" (similar check, like in credit card numbers).
6. This is your public address.

"Nerd-mode OFF" :-)

this with 34 characters:

1HFSx5TPYYzQTQmBXeJNcMhUDT6FNGF11q

(This address is a random address, so do NOT send any funds there).

WHAT DOES OPEN SOURCE MEAN?

Open source means that the actual code of how a program or blockchain is written is publicly available and can be accessed and checked by anyone. This allows others to do checks, advise on improvements, and also warn if services are faulty or malicious. In blockchain and cryptocurrencies, this aspect is essential to an open and inclusive community.

WHY DO WE NEED PRIVATE KEYS AND PUBLIC ADDRESSES?

This system is 100% inclusive. It literally allows anyone, or even anything, to join a community with a blockchain. Nothing and no one can block you, as all you have to do is generate a private key and derive the public address from it. Looking back at some of the advantages of a decentralized currency, it becomes clear how valuable this feature is, especially looking at regions in the world where traditional banking systems are still very limited. Anyone is allowed to know your public address ("your email address") so you can receive money, but your private key (like your email password) is needed to send money associated with a public address. Just like anyone can send an email to you, but only the person with the password to that email can send emails from that account. Yes, some hackers try to fake that with phishing emails, but you get the point.

The most important lesson to take away from this chapter is:

NEVER, and I mean NEVER EVER EVER EVER give anyone your private key. The person controlling a private key controls the coins that get sent to its public address.

I cannot stress this fact often enough. There are websites that sell you special looking public addresses—for example having your name inside the address, such as 1HFSx5JULIANHOSPXeJNcMhUDT-6FNGF11q. This works by these websites trying trillions of private keys until they find such a special looking public address. While it seems great, there is a huge security risk when using such services, since as soon as someone knows your private key, it is like them knowing your email password.

So, what is next after each participant has one or more accounts to send and receive money in this system? The next thing that has to be solved (and which was a true eye-opener to me personally) is the process of how it is determined how much money actually is in any given account. It is the question we started with in this chapter: How can you avoid a double-spend if no central party watches over these accounts? This is where a process called "mining" comes into play.

CHAPTER 4 – MINING

Mining is one of the most misunderstood things in cryptocurrencies, as most people believe mining is how bitcoins, for example, are created. This is partly incorrect.

WHAT IS MINING?

Mining is the process of how consensus is created.

Consensus is the agreement about how much money is tied to a private key. Basically, how much money is in each participant's account? In a centralized system as we have with fiat money, a central institution like a bank watches over how much money you have and whether you can actually pay for something or not. In decentralized systems, it works by every participant watching everyone else and then either confirming or rejecting a transaction based on whether you have the money or not.

WHAT ARE USERS, NODES AND MINDERS?

Users (many times also called light-nodes): Most of the people in a decentralized network are users. They make and receive payments and have to pay miners a small fee (this fee can also be zero sometimes) for them to check the validity of their transactions.

Full-nodes: Nodes forward information they receive to everyone else, for them to also have the same information, and for the network to stay decentralized.

Miners: Miners check and verify transactions that users want to make. They create consensus.

In theory, anyone can do all three things: mine (check transactions), forward info to others (full-node) and use the system (user). However, these roles are way more specialized. Most people using a cryptocurrency join as a user to send and receive money. They leave it to others (miners) to make sure the transactions are correct and that full-nodes forward the transactions within the network so that everyone has the same information on what the transaction history (blockchain) looks like. Full-nodes are set up as check points and are not really participating in actual transactions. What results is, instead of one central institution, a large group of people creating consensus.

WHAT IS CONSENSUS?

Consensus is agreement over what has and what hasn't happened.

How does this work in a decentralized system as chances are, the more participants (miners) there are, the more disagreement there is? Blockchain technologies have a very elegant solution to creating consensus. As soon as you decide to make a payment to someone, you have to use your private key to "sign" this transaction. This basically means that you send money from one public address to another. Since only you (hopefully!) have the private key associated with the public address, it is only you who can send these coins and no one else. Since there is no central authority watching, you have to broadcast this transaction to a few full-nodes that your wallet is connected to—your wallet does that automatically. Then, these nodes forward this information to other nodes and miners, who do the same thing. This is an exponential wave that happens within a few milliseconds, and soon everyone who is part of the community knows about your transaction.

Whenever a miner receives a transaction, they check whether the transaction was actually correctly signed with the private key and that you had the coins in the first place. Since there are several transactions every second, you can "bribe" the miners to pick and "check" your transaction first, by paying a small fee. In theory, you don't have to pay any fees, but since there are so many transactions happening at the same time, miners would never start to process your transaction to include it into the blockchain (transaction history), as they earn more by processing those transactions that give them a fee. Every legit cryptocurrency has a set of cryptographic rules that make sure that miners cannot make up fake stuff. For example, they cannot just create fake transactions like crediting themselves with millions of dollars.

So, how is it decided which miner gets your fee, since only one miner receives it? Also, what if you tried a double-spending attack by broadcasting one transaction to one miner and a different transaction with the same money to another? Which transaction is valid, and which one is not? Even though there is a democratic system among the miners, if anyone just gets to vote on the transactions as they wish, it is going to be quite chaotic. Also, since all you need for your transaction to be valid is other miners to confirm your transaction, why not create thousands of miners yourself? They, in turn, could confirm that someone sent you millions of dollars. This would be called a sybil attack, and we will talk about it when we talk about attacking cryptocurrencies.

WHAT IS A CONSENSUS ALGORITHM?

In order to avoid all this chaos, legit cryptocurrencies have developed consensus mechanisms that govern the above-mentioned problems in a decentralized system:

1. Conflict of opposing information—one miner saying one thing and another saying something else.
2. Possibility of creating fake miners who work in your interest and allow you to cheat.
3. Incentive mechanisms to motivate as many people in the system to participate in the consensus and not only participating as a user.

While there are many more consensus algorithms in the making and they might be labeled differently in different cryptocurrencies, these are the three most important ones:

1. Proof of Importance
2. Proof of Stake
3. Proof of Work

1. PROOF OF IMPORTANCE

This is one of the least used so far. It might be adopted more in the coming years, but so far Proof of Work has mostly been used. With a Proof of Importance consensus algorithm, the participant with the "most importance" gets to say which transactions happened and also receives incentives the most often. Since the person will not be the only participant with importance, it is a probabilistic mix of when they have authority and when someone else does. How does importance get established? Different cryptocurrencies have different mechanisms for that, but one factor is the length of time someone is part of the system, combined with the number of other miners trusting them by opting in to receive information from them.

Compare it to social media. You are more likely to trust the friend request of someone on Facebook that has been on there for quite some time already, has a legit looking profile, and many of your friends are already connected to this new friend. It is similar in the world of decentralization when Proof of Importance is used. Someone's importance percentage is based on the value the system decides, which assigns how much "voting power" they have, how often they get to go first with transaction processing, and how often they are rewarded. The upside of this system is that literally anyone, poor or rich, can achieve a high level of importance. The downside is that this system could be gamed by simply creating fraudulent participants who then vote for each other, thereby creating importance. See it like a fake social media account that people start to follow only because many others are following it. Few blockchain algorithms are using this mechanism for this reason, and it probably still needs some additional features to scale well.

2. PROOF OF STAKE

The idea of importance can be taken a step further, where money resembles importance. Basically, whoever controls more money in the system has more importance. As you might already imagine, this system has a lot of critics, as it begs the question of how such a network could be decentralized, if only a few rich accounts share all the consensus power. So far, only a few blockchains are using this consensus mechanism, but for those that do, it seems to be working well. The risk of one large player ruling it all is eminent, but the advantages of this system are on the table:

- The mechanism of understanding how much voting power you have is clear by simply dividing the amount of money you stake (proof of your money by locking it in a special contract for a given period of time), with the total amount staked by the community. So, there is the possibility that while someone might have a lot of money, they may still not have much voting rights because they are spending it on a regular basis and not staking it as proof of his ownership. The math is clear and simple. If you were to stake 1,000 coins, for example, and 100,000 coins are being staked in total, you have 1% voting power and are expected to get 1% of the say and 1% of the rewards.

- Since the rewards of the transaction system get shared with the stakers, whoever puts up more will get a larger percentage of the rewards. Therefore, you can calculate a much more accurate return on your money on an annual basis, which might be an interesting investment opportunity. For example, you know that a blockchain might reward you with 5% of your staked-up capital per year. You stake 1,000 coins and receive 50 coins every year for taking part in the consensus algorithm. Depending on what these coins are worth, this can mean a lot.

- Since money cannot be created out of thin air in a legit blockchain, the possibility of fraudulent attackers, as in proof of importance, is rather low.

Of course, there are also downsides. One of them, besides the rich getting richer, is the risk of forking attacks. We will discuss this a bit later, but to give you a short overview: In proof of stake, if a blockchain forks (splits), you automatically control the coins on both new chains. You just doubled your coins that you can keep staking on either. Developers are still looking for good solutions in that regard.

This is different than proof of work, as here you have to make a decision on which chain you invest your work into.

3. PROOF OF WORK

The last of the three consensus algorithms is the most used and oldest of them all. Most of the large cryptocurrencies use it because it has been tested extensively over the past years, and it is the most resistant to the aforementioned forking attacks. Instead of proving your importance or staking money, you have to prove that you have done work. Whoever does the work first gets to be the first to choose the transaction composition and also gets the mining reward. This reward consists of all the transaction fees of that time frame (block) and, depending on the cryptocurrency, an additional incentive. For example, Bitcoin's incentive is 12.5 bitcoins per block (time frame). Let's dig into

GEEKY

Oltre al motivo morale, per cui con lo stake i ricchi vengono premiati ancora di più, esiste tuttavia anche un drastico svantaggio tecnico: la possibilità di costanti fork (in italiano: ripartizione di una blockchain). Parleremo più avanti in dettaglio di fork, ma vorrei anticipare questo: normalmente per un fork si deve decidere con un algoritmo di consenso, da che parte del fork ci si dirige. Con il proof of stake questo NON è necessario, perché qui si continuano a controllare i coin su entrambe le chain. In questo campo si stanno ancora cercando valide soluzioni.

GEEKY OFF

that concept a bit deeper because it also explains a lot of other important ideas at the same time. We could do this with any other example, but Bitcoin is the oldest and most tested blockchain, so it makes sense to examine the "mother of all cryptocurrencies."

HOW DOES A TRANSACTION GET CONFIRMED?

In Bitcoin, if you want to send bitcoins to someone, it is similar to how the Yap islanders "sent" Rai stones. Instead of actually sending bitcoins, you notify the nodes and miners about who is the new owner of the coins on the blockchain. They then forward this info to others; however, in order to avoid any conflicting information, none of your intentions are confirmed initially—they stay **unconfirmed**. A transaction only gets confirmed once it is included in a so-called "block." In Proof of Stake and Proof of Importance, the time until one of the participants, based on their importance or staking amount, gets to be first to choose which transactions are included, is fixed. For example, every 3 seconds, 60 seconds, or any other arbitrary number set in the blockchain's algorithm. In proof of work, whoever does the work first gets to choose the block's composition first. This is when the transaction is **confirmed** for the first time. Let's look into that from the miners' perspective.

Miners watch the network for broadcasted transactions. As soon as they see one, they add it to their pool of unconfirmed transactions. At the same time, they have to do some work. All this happens with lightning speed and is fully automated in the background. The work they have to do is reverse engineering a difficult cryptographic algorithm, which can only be done by trying over and over again. Imagine it the same as solving a puzzle. Everyone gets a puzzle with a certain number of pieces, and whoever is first to put them together wins. The puzzle pieces represent transactions and consist of a few fixed points, but a lot of variables. For example, one piece is the last puzzle part that was solved first. Every miner is using this same puzzle piece for the new attempt. Next, every miner picks the transactions they want to include in this puzzle and tries to piece it together. Since most blockchains only allow a certain amount of transactions per block, miners have to choose which ones they pick. Most likely, they choose those transactions with the highest fees, as this is what they get to keep on top of the rewards if they win. There are a lot of possibilities, so the chances that different miners are working on different puzzles (which are called blocks) are very high. Blocks/puzzles are structured in a way that they cannot be solved without adding a so-called "nonce."

HOW DO YOU FIND BLOCKS?

A nonce is a random piece that has to be included in a block that every miner has to find. For a nonce to be legit, the finished puzzle needs to look a certain way. Imagine it like this last piece is the missing link for a puzzle not to have any gaps. Depending on how the other puzzle pieces

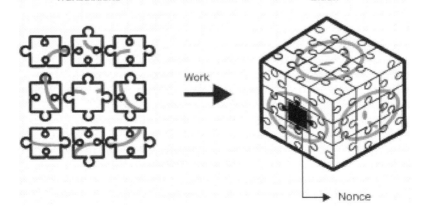

Transactions   Block

Work

Nonce

look and how a miner stacks them together, this nonce needs to have a very specific shape. The problem is that a miner does not see upfront if this last puzzle piece fits or not. They literally try trillions of nonces until they find one that makes the puzzle/block correct. In blockchain language, this is termed **"finding a new block."**

> ### GEEKY
> What the miner actually managed to do is back-calculate several SHA256 cryptographic algorithms by guessing a random input for a fixed output.
> ### GEEKY OFF

Once a miner finds a valid solution, they then broadcast this block to several other nodes and miners, who look at the block/puzzle, make sure it is correct, and only then forward it to others. As you know from your own experience, it takes a fraction of a second to look at a puzzle to see if it is correct or not, but it takes minutes, hours, or even days for someone to build it. If you have ever stared in awe at a puzzle with thousands of pieces, you know what I mean. The same is the case in cryptography with blockchains; it takes every miner quite some time to create the puzzle/block, but only a few milliseconds to check whether someone else's puzzle/block is correct and would be accepted as the next block in the blockchain.

HOW ARE BLOCKS CONNECTED TO A BLOCKCHAIN?

A finished block gets numbered through a timestamp. The miner who found the block gets the transaction fees of all the transactions included in the block and receives a reward on top of that. In the case of Bitcoin, this is the aforementioned 12.5 bitcoins per block (however, it gets less and less over time). If a transaction is part of this block, the transaction is now confirmed for the first time. Within a few milliseconds, many thousands or even millions of miners copy that block and start mining on the new block by using the last puzzle piece of the latest block, adding new transaction puzzle pieces and trying to find a nonce that makes this new puzzle correct. When this new block is found, the next block uses part of the past block and so on. Any new block comes on top of an older block, and this is how the numbering is created.

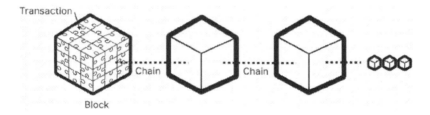

IMPORTANT
Cryptographically speaking, all blocks get chained together, and this is how a blockchain is formed.

The first block in any blockchain is called the **genesis block**. In Bitcoin, it was created by Satoshi on January 3rd, 2009. Today, we have hundreds of thousands of blocks on top of it—all chained together through cryptography. You could not alter any block in the middle, since it would destroy the entire blockchain after that block. This is very important for the understanding of the **immutability of a blockchain**. If you wanted to change the past, you would have to undo all the following blocks (puzzles) and start from scratch. If you just change one single transaction (puzzle piece), the entire puzzle (block) and thereby all the following puzzles (blocks) change. For pretty much all cases, it takes more effort to change the blockchain than there is to gain from altering it.

> **IMPORTANT**
> That is why a blockchain is seen as an immutable transaction history that a decentralized community agrees on.

In the case of Bitcoin, once a transaction has been confirmed 4 or 5 times (3 to 4 other blocks are on top of it), which takes around 40-50 minutes, it is seen as immutable. Practically speaking, a transaction in Bitcoin is pretty safe even if it is only confirmed once, especially if it is a smaller amount. Who would invest a few thousand dollars of computer time, which are the costs to mine a new block, just to steal a few dollars from you? It makes no sense economically speaking, unless you have some really mean friends! In general terms, even a transaction worth hundreds of thousands of dollars is considered immutable after 4 or 5 transactions in Bitcoin, thanks to cryptography.

> **IMPORTANT**
> Remember, in any currency we have to ask the question of why we trust that currency to be a good store of value, method of transfer, and unit of account. We discussed this in the first chapter: **Gold: History. Fiat: Central authority. Crypto: cryptography.**

Obviously, the more people participate in a cryptocurrency, the more stable it gets, as it is incredibly difficult to outwork the rest of the group. If there are just ten people who are part of a cryptocurrency, it is quite fragile, but just imagine you have millions of people, as in the case of Bitcoin. It is very powerful. Every once in a while, groups disagree. A situation where this could happen is if two miners find a block pretty much at the same time.

WHAT ARE ORPHAN BLOCKS?

An **orphan block is a VALID block** that was created when another miner found another VALID block at the same time.

The system has an elegant solution for this. It is programmed for every miner to work on the longest part of the blockchain, as obviously this is the chain where the most work has been put into. If two miners find a block at the same time, there are two parts of a blockchain that have the same length. The miners therefore split into two groups for a brief part and mine on different ends. One group most likely wins by finding the next block first and has the longest chain again. All the miners then shift to that chain, and the block that is left out becomes a so-called orphan block. Such orphan blocks are not a big problem because most transactions in that block will also have been included in the other block, and if not, they will be in one of the next confirmations anyways. This is why it is recommended to only see something as truly confirmed after a few blocks/confirmations have happened.

WHAT IS MINING DIFFICULTY?

In the entire cryptocurrency's network, millions of computers try several trillion times a second to find the solution to a block. Since this is pure probability when someone actually finds the right nonce, it is possible to make mathematical predictions for when this happens. For example, the Bitcoin algorithm adapts the **mining difficulty** (the difficulty of the puzzle) every 2016 blocks to a time window, where it takes the entire network around 10 minutes (= 600 seconds) to solve a block. Since the amount of hashing power goes up exponentially, the mining difficulty does so as well. Different cryptocurrencies use different mining difficulties, which is one of the things that set them apart. Bitcoin does that by forcing the miners to create blocks (puzzles) that look a certain way. To be specific, they have to find a nonce, so the resulting block hash has starts with a certain number of zeros. The more zeros are required, the harder it is to mine. That is how the mining difficulty is adjusted.

Essentially, the mining difficulty adjusts to the network's hashrate.

WHAT IS A HASHRATE?

The hashrate is the number of attempts one manages to achieve per second to find the right nonce to solve a block.

To put that into perspective, a human being has a hashrate of around 0.00003 H/s (hashes per second). This means, if someone tries mining by hand (solving a puzzle), it would take them around 9-10 hours to try 1 nonce (trying 1 puzzle piece to complete the puzzle). In Bitcoin, the total number of attempts to solve a block is calculated as the total hashrate of the network. This number is up in the millions of trillions per second (= tera hashes) and can be followed live here: https://blockchain.info/charts/hash-rate. These are insanely large numbers: 10,000,000,000,000,000,000 hashes per second. Compare that to a human being of 0.00003… The odds of finding a block can simply be calculated by dividing your hashrate by the total hashrate of the network. As a human, you would have to try for a very very very long time, and the more popular a cryptocurrency gets, the more miners join in to try their chance. That's why the hashing power has been and will keep going up exponentially over time.

WHAT ARE THE DIFFERENT TYPES OF MINERS?

At the very beginning, Satoshi (the person or group inventing Bitcoin) probably mined bitcoins with his personal computer completely alone. He owned 100% of the hashrate. Over time, other miners joined, sharing the hashrate and therefore the rewards. The more attractive mining became, the better and more specific the computers became that were used for mining. Today, normal computers cannot really be used anymore for such huge amounts of calculations as the machines have become incredibly specialized. Here is a rough overview of mining equipment:

1. The CPU (Central Processing Unit) in your regular pc or laptop will have a hashrate of 1-3 million per second, depending on how many MHz it has. This sounds like a lot, but if you calculate the odds of winning at the current total hashrate, you will realize that you would spend way more on electricity to run the computer than you would gain from the rewards. Even if electricity was free, you would wear down your computer before you would see any meaningful income

2. GPU mining (Graphical Processing Unit) came next. Using your graphical processor is a lot more effective, as it has been found that these units are way more efficient in solving hashes when comparing hashing output with time and electricity cost. For example, many Radeons have hashrates of 30-50 million per second. That's around 20x more efficient than a normal CPU. That is because a CPU has to be able to do a whole lot of other things, while your graphical processor is already more specialized.

3. ASIC miners (Application-specific Integrated Circuit) are computers that do nothing else than hash faster than any other computer can. That's all they can do. If they cannot hash Bitcoin blocks, you can throw them away. Think about that; there are companies who invest millions into factories that produce nothing other than ASIC machines for mining. That's their entire business model, and it is huge. For example, Bitmain, which produces the famous Antminer that owns the majority of the Bitcoin miner production, is probably a billion-dollar company. These ASIC miners can do several giga- and sometimes even terahashes per second. Giga means a billion and tera a trillion. These are insanely large numbers. Blockchains such as Ethereum and many others are trying to keep the mining within the range of GPU mining though. That way, no specialized equipment can be built, and decentralization is kept strong.

IS MINING PROFITABLE?

For the average person, it makes very little sense to mine. Taking the equipment and electricity cost into account, the output one gets from the block rewards and transaction fees is most often a negative cash-flow business. Obviously, most mining equipment producers or cloud mining providers (companies where you pay others to mine for you) want you to join and try to make their calculations look very profitable for you, while in reality they are a break-even endeavor at best. Considering the exponential increase in difficulty, in pretty much all cases I have ever looked into, it makes way more sense to invest in the coin directly rather than the mining. For example, a CPU might make you a few USD a year—yes, a year! A GPU maybe 50 USD. An ASIC miner can make you a few hundred USD a year, but you need to take electricity and equipment costs into account. All these numbers are mere examples and actually decrease the higher the total hashrate gets.

IMPORTANT

The profit in mining consists of the mining reward plus all transaction (Tx) fees during the block period.

Why do so many people still try their luck in mining? Two words: certainty and passive income. People love both. They love to invest, believing they will receive a fixed sum every month. The reality is less lucrative when you consider the cost to buy your equipment and paying for electricity (unless you smoosh it from someone illegally). It is also certain that your payouts will go down every month, since the total hashrate keeps going up. If it didn't go up, it would actually mean the cryptocurrency is losing popularity, which is completely bad. The way large mining companies stay profitable is by negotiating extremely good hardware and electricity prices, usually managing a 10-15% net profit margin. Meaning, if they invest 1 million USD, they make around 100,000 to 150,000 USD per year. Just for comparison, since Bitcoin's beginnings in 2009, Bitcoin went up more than the 15% in all those years except for 2014. It would have been a way better investment to invest into Bitcoin directly, rather than into mining. Pretty much all other coins follow a similar pattern. So whenever someone offers you a "great income opportunity" by mining a coin, thank them, stay away, and instead consider investing in the coins directly. For large corporations, certainty of a return is more important than the actual amount, since this is the only way they can have positive cashflow and pay employees every month. The average person however, should only get into mining for experimentation and not for investment purposes.

ARE THERE ECONOMIC MINING SOLUTIONS?

As you might have already guessed, Proof of Work mining is one of the most wasteful processes from an energy point of view. Millions of dollars of electricity are being spent to create consensus. This is definitely not an environmentally friendly system. There have been multiple attempts to have miners solve "puzzles" that could actually be used in real life. Possibilities include DNA recombination calculations, prime number searches, and much more. While some have appeared to be promising for a while, the fact that such puzzles would have to have a consistent difficulty plus a puzzle following another had to be just as random as the puzzle before, the search for real life applications has not been all too fruitful… yet. There are hopes that soon real-world problems could be solved during the mining process. The fact that so much stress is being put on our planet with Proof of Work mining is also part of the reason why many blockchains have been pushing towards a Proof of Stake consensus or something similar.

The concept of everyone in the network storing all this information to crosscheck the validity of a new transaction brought up a relevant question: How should everyone be able to store all that data? Isn't that a whole lot of information? There is a solution to this: SPV.

WHAT IS A SPV (SIMPLE PAYMENT VERIFICATION)?

It has been shown, that you do NOT need to know the entire block-chain (all puzzle pieces of a puzzle) to verify a transaction. You can actually leave out a lot, as long as you leave enough pieces in so the remaining spaces can be "assumed." In reality, this works by only having to check some parts of the resulting hash of a block (merkle tree root) and not every entry, since they become a logical consequence. To put this into a picture, imagine a puzzle where pieces are missing. As long as there are enough other pieces left, you can pretty confidently predict whether a new piece that I show to you could fit or not. You don't know the exact information, but you can exclude a lot of possibilities. This fact allows you to verify whether someone actually has the money he is trying to send you or not.

SPV

 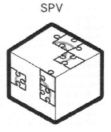

The size of data can then often be reduced to 1/1,000 of its original size. This means "only" a few hundred mega- instead of gigabytes need to be stored, which is a lot more reasonable. This is how simple payment verification works. SPV only works, of course, if enough other people store the full blockchain on servers for full verification, but it allows mobile users or so-called light-wallets to keep data and processing to a minimum. Aside of SPV, blockchain technologies bet on data storage and processing to increase. Gigabytes might soon only be as "large" as megabytes today.

Another important feature of a financial system aside of the storage size is how many transactions (Tx) can be processed per second.

WHAT IS THE SCALING DEBATE?

Most credit card companies, for example, transact around 2,000 transactions per second. This is where blockchain technologies still have a major limitation: Since every node in the network needs to keep a record of the entire network, the speed of the network is limited by the speed of the slowest node. Blockchains limit the amount of transactions per second to avoid a centralization of the computing power by large and strong nodes, which can store and process these larger blocks, but also to keep the blockchain's size from blowing up too fast. Some of the most heated discussions in the crypto-community are about the suggested block size with its upside being the ability to allow for more Tx/s. However, that brings with it the downsides of storage and processing capabilities.

Bitcoin for example allows for around 6-7 Tx/s, Ethereum around 15 Tx/s. In Bitcoin, a miner therefore gets around 4,200 puzzle pieces to fit every 10 minutes into a puzzle (7 Tx/s * 60s * 10min = 4,200 Tx per block). Such a block in Bitcoin takes up 1MB of space. If you wanted to store more Tx within a block, you either have to make the size of a transaction smaller (less data per Tx), or you increase the blocksize (more data stored). SegWit solves that partially from the size angle.

WHAT IS SEGWIT?

In August 2017, Bitcoin introduced an update called Segregated Witness, or short—SegWit—to improve Bitcoin's scaling. If you remember the puzzle piece analogy of a cryptocurrency transaction, you remember that half the puzzle is the transaction information itself and the other half is the signature of the private key. With the SegWit update, the transactions got structured in a different manner, where now the signature was taken away and stored "segregated." Instead of needing an area of the puzzle piece to store the signature, which is only needed for verification and not for actual information, it can now be stored differently, for example as a type of color on the piece itself. That's why it is called a "segregated witness." Since the puzzle pieces are now only half the original size (the signature is not taking up space anymore), twice as many SegWit transactions can be stored in the same 1 MB block (around 8,400 SegWit puzzle pieces fit into a complete puzzle).

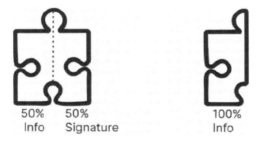

50%   50%   100%
Info   Signature   Info

For the user, SegWit is a soft-fork, meaning they can still send the old transaction format, just like they can use an older version of WhatsApp and newer versions can still understand them. "Old" Bitcoin addresses for example start with a "1," SegWit addresses start with a "3." It will take a few more months until the full storage capabilities are being utilized and, of course, the blocksize and therefore the scaling debate of Bitcoin will continue.

WHAT ARE POTENTIAL SCALING SOLUTIONS?

No one knows what the ultimate scaling solution will look like, but there are already some promising "proof of concepts." A newer type of distributed ledger called IOTA uses a localized tangle. Another option is a hashgraph that is based on "gossip." Both remove the need of a complete blockchain all together. A group of Bitcoin is working on the Lightning Network and a group of Ethereum on Raiden. Both solutions allow for grouping of users "off-chain," where the members of this group trust each other and can do transactions in a secure manner, without having to inform everyone else in the network.

These are just some of the potential solutions and I will cover more in the chapter on coins and technologies at the end. We have now covered all the steps that happen in a blockchain transaction, so let's put them together to form a full picture as a summary in a grand finale, which you could use anytime to explain to a 10-year-old how a blockchain or cryptocurrency works:

HOW TO EXPLAIN A BLOCKCHAIN TRANSACTION TO A 10-YEAR-OLD?

1. In order to make a transaction, you need to prove that you actually own these funds. You do this with your private key.
2. You create a transaction, which we call a puzzle piece.
3. Half of the puzzle piece is the information, who you are sending however many coins.
4. The other half of the puzzle piece is your signature with your key.
5. Both halves make the puzzle piece completely unique. If you changed either half, it would look completely different, become invalid and can only be reproduced by knowing the ori-

ginal information of private key, sender, and receiver.

6. This transaction gets broadcast to the network. While it is impossible to be reproduced by someone without the original info, it is very easy to verify whether the puzzle piece is correct. Is the signature correct? Is the information of "from" and "to" correct? Are the timestamps valid? Etc.

7. Miners pick up the transactions and try to find a block by finding a merkle root that starts with a certain number of zeros. This is called mining, and we described it as putting the puzzle pieces together to form a correct puzzle.

8. It takes the entire network around 10 minutes in the case of Bitcoin (other blockchains take different amount of times) to solve the puzzle through sheer luck.

9. Once a miner finds a valid block, they broadcast it to everyone, who can then verify the correctness within milliseconds.

10. The puzzle gets "fixed" and is connected to the puzzle from before without being able to be altered.

11. These blocks form a chain and are called a blockchain, which consists of all the transactions ever made. Any new transaction (puzzle piece) starts at step 1. It needs to be connected and checked for its validity within this blockchain so it can be picked up by miners, which is why one needs to know the entire blockchain. History cannot be altered as it would destroy the blocks and thereby the chain.

Simple overview, right? A blockchain explained to a 10-year-old. :-)

WHAT DOES A BLOCKCHAIN LOOK LIKE IN REALITY?

Time to get a bit geeky again. Are you ready for the reality? What if I told you there were no puzzle pieces, no blocks, and no chains. Mind blown, right? ;-) It's all nothing but cryptography, which is only strings of digits. You own your private key—a string of digits. This private key signs (a cryptographic function where your private key gets combined with a string, thereby creating a completely new unique string) a transaction ID, another number, which consists of other numbers, such as time, from, to, amount, etc.

Again, all numbers and strings that get cryptographically connected together. The result of the signing is a completely unique string, since no one else has your private key, and considering time, from, to, and amount, it is all unique. That is why every puzzle piece looks different and no one can back-calculate from a puzzle piece to the private key. Miners now pick up these transactions (strings), verify them against the public address the coins are being sent from (more strings), and hash all the different numbers into one single string, while getting as many zeros in the resulting string as needed. This is putting the puzzle pieces together, while checking the mining difficulty. One of the pieces that needs to be hashed into this so-called merkle root is the string of the block before, which is completely unique again. Therefore, if you changed the string of the block before (by changing any of the transactions) or any of the other puzzle pieces, the resulting puzzle (block hash) would look completely different.

IMPORTANT

What results from all the cryptographic functions is a completely random string of digits and numbers... That is called a blockchain.

Mind = blown? It was for me when I understood all that for the

---

very first time. The terms blocks, blockchain, etc. are all just a figure of speech of what is really happening on a cryptographic level. Now that we have covered account management and sending and receiving of coins in a decentralized system, let's discuss how cryptocurrencies are created in the first place.

CHAPTER 5 – HOW ARE CRYPTOCURRENCIES CREATED?

Controlling the supply of a currency is the responsibility of a central authority in a centralized system. In a decentralized system, the cryptographic algorithm sets the rules for the creation, and all participants agree to it. As I mentioned in the mining chapter: People believe mining is there for a cryptocurrency to be created, but actually there are several ways for that to happen. Remember, mining is to create consensus… And in the case of Bitcoin, to also create bitcoins. There are, however, several other options on how this could work. Let's look at the most important ones.

1. MINING: We covered this one already and in its case, cryptocurrencies get created during the consensus process. It is a very common process as it incentivizes participants to help with stabilizing the network. Bitcoin is the most famous example for this application, and initially 50 bitcoins were rewarded per block to its finder. A so-called **halving** takes place every 210,000 blocks, which takes around four years, where the block reward is halved. So, when Bitcoin started in 2009 it was 50 bitcoins, then in 2012 it became 25 bitcoins and since 2016 we only have 12.5 bitcoins per block. Sometime in 2020, depending on how long the next 210,000 blocks take, we will have the next halving to 6.25 bitcoins per block. This happens for a total of 64 times, which is the time when Bitcoin reaches a mining reward of its smallest unit, a Satoshi, which cannot be halved anymore. This will occur theoretically in the year 2140; however, depending on the hashrate, it could potentially happen a bit earlier.

In the case of Bitcoin, close to 21 million bitcoins will be created that way and distributed over the network in a more or less fair manner. Info for extra credit: it is actually slightly less than 21 million bitcoins, because just like when halving a distance over and over again, you never actually reach the end (1/2 + ¼ + 1/8 + 1/16 +…never actually reaches 1, but gets super super close;). However, in Bitcoin language, we disregard that and state:

The maximum supply of bitcoins is 21 million.

2. PRE-MINED: In this version, every coin has been created when the cryptocurrency started. As long as this does NOT happen on a legitimate public and open source blockchain, this can be considered a SCAM, as all the creator is doing is creating a new centralized system, while calling it a cryptocurrency. Sadly, many con artists trick people out of millions of dollars on a regular basis that way. Most (NOT all!) Initial Coin Offerings (ICOs), token sales, and many others use this version in a legitimate way to create all the coins and then sell them to the market. As a rule of thumb: if the creators of a pre-mined cryptocurrency can be seen manipulating the market, the coin should be treated with caution. We will talk about these use cases in great detail at a later stage in the altcoin chapter.

3. A MIX OF PRE-MINED AND MINING: Some coins—like Ethereum—which is one of the largest crypto-assets as of the writing of this book, use a hybrid-model of option 1 and 2. It starts with a pre-mined amount but has a mining model afterwards, as well. The total supply can be capped, as it is with Ethereum Classic at around 210 million ETC, or uncapped, as it is with the other (traditional) Ethereum. Both models work, and only the future will tell which one is better from an economic perspective.

WHAT IS A DEFLATIONARY CURRENCY?

Some people see the maximum limit of a cryptocurrency as the reason on why it is better than fiat currencies, which can be inflated by a central authority to infinity. Others see it as the problem, as they call it a deflationary currency, because people will very likely lose their private keys over time and thereby access to the coins, which means the number of circulating bitcoins is decreasing, thereby deflationary. However, here is why both beliefs are incorrect.

DO ALL CRYPTOCURRENCIES HAVE A CAPPED SUPPLY?

Some cryptocurrencies have an uncapped supply by having a fixed annual inflation rate of 3% of the total supply, for example. There are also systems where participants get to vote on reward percentages, almost like a democratic inflation system. Such structures would still make a cryptocurrency better than a fiat currency, since the algorithm is public and can be seen and trusted by everyone. Therefore, if you want to sound smart in cryptocurrencies, never sell the fact of Bitcoin having a hard cap as an advantage over fiat currencies. Honestly, no one today knows if a currency with a few percent inflation is better or worse than a currency with a complete hard cap. The future will tell. The true advantage is the AUTHENTICITY and FAIRNESS of the rules, compared to that of a centralized one.

IS A DEFLATIONARY CURRENCY PROBLEMATIC?

What about the argument that many cryptocurrencies are deflationary and deflation has been shown by people holding their coins instead of spending them, thereby not making such a currency a good means of transfer? This is a valid argument; however, putting those coins with an inherent inflation aside, which would invalidate this argument, one still needs to see the ability to split these coins into smaller parts. Just like the dollar has cents, so do many coins. 1 bitcoin has 10^8 Satoshis (100 million). So, if we assumed a complete equal distribution of bitcoins over around 8 billion people, everyone could own 21M * 100M / 8B = 262,500 Satoshis per person. Assuming that access to half of all the coins will get lost over time, which might be realistic, there are still 131,250 Satoshis left for every person, which is more than enough to give it a good value to work as a method of transfer.

Obviously, a coin that has a fixed hard cap will appreciate in value way more when people start using it more, compared to a coin that is constantly inflating. That does NOT mean that Bitcoin will always go up in value, but it is part of the reason why it has done so in the past and will likely do in the future. More about investing into cryptocurrencies at a later stage though.

CHAPTER 6 – WALLETS

You might be wondering where and how you can store your crypto-currencies. However, the correct question is: How can you store your private key safely?

WHAT IS A WALLET?

In cryptocurrencies, you CANNOT store coins. Coins are always recorded on the blockchain and never move away from there. You use so-called WALLETS to store the private key that lets you send the coins by signing a cryptographic function on the blockchain.

WHAT IS IN A WALLET?

Many people confuse that and talk about having "this many coins in a wallet." What they actually mean is that they have **the keys to a certain amount of coins** in their wallet. It also means that if you ever lose a wallet, you don't necessarily lose your funds… As long as you have written down your private keys somewhere else, you can access them from another wallet anytime.

WHAT ARE DIFFERENT WALLET TYPES?

- Paper-wallet
- Mind-wallet
- Sof- wallet
- Hard-wallet
- Exchanges

WHAT IS A PAPER-WALLET?

Back in 2009, when Bitcoin was just starting, the very first private keys were simply created by a random number generator and then written down on a piece of paper. They were called paper-wallets, because the private keys were stored on paper. Paper-wallets still exist today and are considered some of the most secure ways of storing your private keys. I only recommend using paper-wallets as a so-called offline back-up or cold-storage for large coin amounts, as it is not worth the hassle otherwise, as you will learn in a second.

HOW TO CREATE A PAPER-WALLET

- Write your private key or seed **WITH A PENCIL** on strong clear paper. Do NOT use a pen as it might dissolve over time. Remember, these keys need to survive as long as coins are connected to it, which might be decades.
- Best is to write the same key or seed on three or four **different papers and put these papers into different locations**. Consider natural disasters or a break in. Put one into a safe, another into a bank, etc.

- NEVER, let me repeat, **NEVER, make a digital copy of a paper-wallet**. This defeats the purpose of such a so-called offline or cold-storage that cannot be accessed by technological means. If a digital copy exists, it can be accessed somehow. So, don't take pictures, don't photocopy it, etc.
- When you write your private key down, only change something in it if you can be **100% certain** that you will remember what you changed, even in ten years.

A friend of mine, for example, thought he was extra smart by changing one of the words of his seed when writing it down on paper. He thought that if anyone were to find this paper it would be worthless because it would only be him knowing what piece got changed. Well, what happened was, when he needed the private key a few months later, he had already forgotten which word he changed into what. He kept trying and trying but could not remember anymore. Gladly he did not have too many coins associated with that private key, but it was still a painful experience.

WHAT IS A MIND-WALLET?

In a **mind-wallet**, the complete key is memorized and not written down anywhere.

WHAT ARE OFFLINE-WALLETS?

Mind- and paper-wallets are considered offline wallets as they cannot be accessed by the internet. If you ever want to use the keys in your paper- or mind-wallet, you insert the private key into an online-wallet, from where you can then actually send your coins. As soon as you do that, your offline-wallet is online. In order to stay offline, you have to clear the old offline-wallet and move all the coins to a new offline-wallet.

WHAT ARE ONLINE-WALLETS?

Around 2010/2011, people got tired of these unhandy paper-wallets and created wallets that were always online. These were called soft(ware)-wallets.

WHAT ARE SOFT-WALLETS?

In a soft-wallet, the private key gets encoded with a password on a computer or app, and one can receive and send money through this application without the cumbersome import and execution function of offline-wallets. Such soft-wallets are obviously not as secure as paper-wallets, since anything that is connected to a computer and especially to the internet is prone to be hacked. (Remember, it is not the blockchain that gets hacked, but your device). Still, they are way more convenient, and if you make sure that you use a difficult password and you NEVER copy the private key anywhere, they are quite good.

IMPORTANT
NEVER make digital copies or screenshots of your private key. You have to treat this key as money because this is what it is.

In order to get the best out of both worlds (offline security and online convenience) two companies—Ledger and Trezor—started to create hard-wallet

WHAT ARE HARD-WALLETS?

Hard-wallets are like a USB stick but with a very important feature: They store the private key in the USB drive, but it cannot be accessed from a computer and thereby also not by the internet. This is really important, as a few charlatans try to sell people regular USB sticks (that can of course be accessed from the computer) for the price of these hard-wallets. I use this specific hard wallet, and I would recommend you too invest the 80-100 USD for this device if you want to start investing in cryptocurrencies: www.julianhosp.com/hardwallet.

The reason hard-wallets are so good is because your private key stays offline at all times. You can only access the private key with a PIN that you actually have to physically enter on the device. Should you ever lose the device, no one can use it, as they do not know the PIN.

WHAT IS COLD-STORAGE?

Cold-storage is when there is NO direct access to the internet:

- Mind-wallets
- Paper-wallets
- Hard Wallets (Ledger, Trezor)

WHAT IS HOT-STORAGE?

Hot-storage is when there IS direct access to the internet:
- Light- SPV-wallet (was discussed in the chapter about Mining)
- Soft-wallet as WebApp
- Soft-wallet as App on phone
- Soft-wallet on computer

Hot-storages are used for convenience; however, they do have some risk because as soon as anyone gets access to your device either through hacking or phishing, they have access to your private key. I do use soft-wallets for small amounts, especially on my phone as it allows me to have these amounts ready anytime without needing a hardware device. Remember to treat your private key or seed like money, because that is what it is. Just because it is only a string of letters or words does not mean it is worthless. It can actually be worth millions.

WHAT IF YOU LOSE YOUR WALLET?

I was once travelling and my hard wallet, which was plugged into my computer, got pressed down by a book on top of it. The book "entered" a wrong PIN three times in a row and so the device completely reset. The only way I could get access to my funds again was by typing in the private key. The paper of my private key was hidden in a secret location out of my reach at that time, and I urgently needed to have access to my funds. So, I called my dad and guided him to where the paper was. Now came the problem—how would he be able to give me the seed consisting of 24 words without any potential "man-in-the-middle- attack," where someone was eavesdropping the key. We used a mix of video, audio, and different writing channels until I had all 24 words. I typed them into my hardware wallet and voila, I had access to my funds again. The first thing I did was to send the money to a new public address (with a new private key), so that in case anyone got to hear about the private key that my dad gave me, they would no longer have access. What this story shows is the importance of treating your key like cash. It also shows that a few things in blockchain, especially the storage (and also the inheritance) of private keys, is not as easy as it will probably become in the future.

IMPORTANT
You can NEVER LOSE your coins. Coins can NEVER get lost. They always stay on the blockchain. You can lose the private key that gives you access to these coins. If you have written down the private key as a paper-wallet as well, you can just buy a new hardware wallet and enter the private key, and you have access to all your funds again.

WHAT IF YOU DO NOT CONTROL THE PRIVATE KEY:

It is very important to understand that if you are using services where you do not know your private key, you are not actually in control of your money. The company you entrust your private keys with is. In return, they provide a typical "login-password" user interface that makes it easy for people to send cryptocurrencies to other people, since this is what they are used to from sites like PayPal, etc. If you do this out of convenience, like on an exchange, etc. then it is okay, as long as you know what you are getting into. Here are some examples:

- Exchanges (where you can change cryptocurrencies among each other or into fiat currencies)
- Private-wallets from companies
- 3rd party providers that facilitate the access to cryptocurrencies by offering a "PayPal-like experience"

I also store small amounts in some of these services. I do this either because I want to have some liquidity ready to buy or sell certain cryptocurrencies, or because the hassle of downloading and installing a soft-wallet is too complicated in comparison to the small amount I own of a specific coin. For example, I might buy a small amount of a coin to test it, but I don't want to deal with new software. So, I just use 3rd party software like an exchange. We will talk about exchanges a bit more at the end when I talk about the easiest ways to actually get yourself some cryptocurrencies.

WHAT ARE DETERMINISTIC WALLETS?

When you start using most of the above mentioned soft- or hard-wallets, you will notice a rather strange feature: Whenever you receive money to an address, the address changes when you want to receive money again. Imagine it this way: Every time you receive money to your bank account, a completely new account opens where your new money goes. This might confuse you at first, as this never happens to a bank account, nor does your e-mail address change after receiving an email.

First, I want to explain the two reasons why these so-called deterministic wallets exist and then how this works from a technical standpoint.

WHY DOES YOUR ADDRESS KEEP CHANGING?

This feature of deterministic wallets was implemented in Bitcoin during a so-called **Bitcoin Improvement Proposal (BIP)**, which are small improvements to the original Bitcoin code, to provide extra security but also convenience. In this case, it was BIP32 (number 32 of the BIPs), where the following was suggested: should there ever ever ever, in the super most unlikely case, happen to be an address collision where two parties receive the same address (which is nigh impossible, but to improve the safety even further), then any person would now own one address with all the coins on it. However, if the funds automatically get split over hundreds or thousands of addresses, you have a certain amount of risk mitigation. Also in the case of a phishing attempt, an attacker would thereby not access to all but only part of the funds.

The second reason is that of privacy and protection of identity, which is a topic we will discuss in a later chapter. To give you a short glimpse, the more addresses you control, the harder it is for an outsider to know how much money you own; therefore, privacy is improved.

WHAT IS A SEED?

In order to do this deterministic key generation, we need an initial instruction. This initial instruction is called a seed and generally consists of 8, 12, or 24 words. These words become the instructions on how to find the first, and then all the following private keys. If you know the instruction, it is very easy to get to the keys, but you could never (or very unlikely) go backwards. For example, imagine that the instruction says that the next private key is always the current private key plus the sum of all its digits. This is not how it actually works because the actual sequence happens through a very complex cryptographic function, but the principle is the same.

<u>Example:</u>

Imagine the second private key (I won't tell you the first one yet) is 3628. What was the first private key in this deterministic sequence? Even though this one would already be quite doable to back-calculate, you probably take a bit to figure out it was 3614. Why 3614? Because adding the digits to the private key (3+6+1+ 4 = 14) gets you from 3614 + 14 to 3628.

What a deterministic wallet basically does is start from the seed that is converted to the first key (in our random example 3614). It then applies the rule and checks all the private keys that get generated through this algorithm, whether coins are associated to it or not. In our case it would be 3614, 3628, 3647,... It stops checking at a certain number of keys, when a predetermined number of keys has no coins connected to it. This could be, for example, 100 keys. So, if the 9th key still had coins on it at some point, it would check until the 109th key if none of the other keys had coins connected to it. The wallet then displays the number of coins as one number, as this is what you have access to.

Don't think that this deterministic sequence is increasing the risk of a collision of people ever creating the same to private keys. Remember, even if you generated a trillion new addresses a nanosecond, and everyone and everything on Earth would have done that since the beginning of the planet (roughly 4.5 billion years ago), it would still be more likely that the universe would just implode than two addresses be the same. Don't you love math? :-)

IMPORTANT

Since the wallet automatically checks all the private keys, you CAN send coins to an "old" or "new" address that is shown in the wallet. You will still get them, as long as an address was ever shown within that specific sequence. So, don't send coins to a different outside address, of course.

CAN YOU HACK A BLOCKCHAIN?

When people ask this question, they mostly hear about people who have had their private keys stolen through a hacking or phishing attack. You can NOT hack a blockchain, as the cryptography is 100% safe. The biggest problem is improperly storing private keys that leads to people losing access to their coins. Personally, I see the inconvenience of storing private keys as one of the major challenges to cryptocurrencies being mass adopted.

If you freak out right now and get scared about getting into the crypto ecosystem, don't worry. First of all, the private key problem is being worked on, and many exchanges are becoming more and more secure, even though you do not control your private key there. I would never recommend leaving too much money on an exchange, but statistically speaking, more access to coins has been lost OFF exchanges than on. This means that more people screwed up handling their own private keys, rather than lost access to funds on exchanges. The reason why most people only hear about funds being lost on exchanges is the same as with car and plane accidents. Planes are way safer than cars, however when a plane crashes, the entire world knows about it—we don't hear much about the millions of people that die in car accidents every year. Same with exchanges versus the self-handling of private keys.

We have now covered most of the ground on what blockchain and cryptocurrencies are, how mining works, and what wallets are. So now let's dig into some of the problems blockchains might face.

CHAPTER 7 – BLOCKCHAIN FORKS AND ATTACKS

Since a blockchain is a community effort, every once in a while, part of that community disagrees with what should be happening. We covered this in the orphan blocks part as regular occurring incidents. However, the community can do this in a more organized manner by either trying to fork (split) the blockchain into two strands to implement ideas or by attacking the blockchain as a whole. Let's talk about so-called forks first and cover attacks afterwards.

WHAT IS A FORK?

A fork means that consensus in a blockchain community gets split into two or more due to a more or less radical change to the underlying protocol.

Whenever an update to the original blockchain code is proposed, either a soft- or a hard-fork has to be initiated in order for these changes to go into effect. Sometimes it can be about something small like a simple update, but sometimes it is about something huge, like a totally new coin supply.

WHAT IS A SOFT-FORK?

A soft-fork works more like an update to the existing protocol. Older versions are still accepted, but these older versions will lack certain newer features. To use a more familiar example, when WhatsApp gets updated, but you decide NOT to update, all it means is you might not be able to use some new features. You will NOT lose your friends, and you can still use the communication you are used to. The same is the case for a soft-fork.

A soft-fork works like a new update and is BACKWARDS COMPATIB-LE. Therefore, the blockchain normally does NOT fork into different strands.

There are exceptions to the forking part, as the Bitcoin example showed in August 2017 with SegWit (Segregated Witness). SegWit was such a soft-fork (update) to the Bitcoin protocol. For the user it was a soft-fork, however, it had a few features included that would have completely forked all miners that did not upgrade to the new consensus. That was more of an exception to the rule and generally speaking, such soft-forks happen on a regular basis to improve the functionality of a blockchain.

WHAT IS A HARD-FORK?

A hard-fork works in a more drastic way. To use the WhatsApp example from before, imagine your friends are unhappy with a few features in WhatsApp, but instead of updating it, they decide to use a completely new app. This is a true split/fork, because you have to decide which group you want to belong to—WhatsApp, the new app, or both. If your friends don't want to use both, you will have to choose because these apps are NOT compatible with each other.

A hard-fork causes a fork/split of a blockchain because a newly suggested upgrade is NOT backwards compatible with its previous version.

Hard-forks occur quite rarely, but if they do, they attract massive attention, because people have to decide which way they want to go. A famous hard-fork happened on the Ethereum blockchain in July 2016, after an attacker managed to steal close to 70 million USD worth of Ether out of a digital smart contract in June 2016. While part of the community decided to hard-fork to "undo" the attack, another part stated that "code is law," meaning, even if what happened is not desirable, it should not be tampered with, as the blockchain code was agreed upon in the first place. What resulted was a fork into Ethereum (ETH) and Ethereum Classic (ETC). Ironically, the actual fork that split off to change history kept the original name Ethereum.

WHAT HAPPENS TO YOUR COINS DURING A FORK?

During a fork, it is especially important that you control the private keys yourself and you haven't outsourced them to an exchange or another 3rd party. Since both new forks build on top of the history of the old chain, your keys will control the coins on BOTH chains now. This always causes a bit of confusion, but if you remember that you never have coins in your wallet, only the keys that point to the coins, it gets clearer. Since the history is the same on both strands, after a fork, you control the coins on both chains, since they were associated with these keys initially. In the described example of Ethereum, if you had 1 ETH before the fork, you now had 1 ETC and 1 ETH after the fork.

The value of these new coins is all about supply and demand and has a lot to do with how much faith the community has in either coin. Normally, if the value of a coin was 10 USD before, the sum of both forked coins should still be 10 USD afterwards.

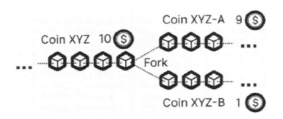

Considering some of the problems that happen during the fork, many times, the total value afterwards is less than it was before.

WHY DOESN'T EVERY FORK GIVE PEOPLE NEW COINS?

On October 7th, 2011, Charlie Lee, a former Google employee, suggested to fork the Bitcoin code by having a few new implementations. In this new blockchain called Litecoin, blocks should take only ¼ of the time of that of Bitcoin (2.5 minutes in Litecoin vs. 10 minutes in Bitcoin), the maximum supply was lifted to four times the amount (84 million litecoins vs. 21 million bitcoins), and a new mining algorithm (Scrypt in Litecoin vs. SHA256 in Bitcoin) was implemented—just to name a few of the updates. Obviously, this was NOT compatible with Bitcoin, so a fork happened. In this case, it actually started with a completely new genesis block (Block Nr. 0), which resulted in people not getting extra coins as Litecoin was forked on a code, not on a blockchain basis. This means that the creator copied and changed the open source code and started with the blockchain from scratch, instead of accepting the entire existing history. Everyone interested in Litecoin had to either participate in mining or buy it from a miner. Charlie Lee did that to have a complete "reset" of the system.

Litecoin is one of the first (the first one was actually Namecoin) and the most famous fork of Bitcoin, and it is still a big player in today's crypto ecosystem. One of the reasons Litecoin survived is probably their change of mining algorithm, which kept Bitcoin miners from attacking the Litecoin chain. How such attacks work in detail we will discuss in a bit.

WHY CAN'T EVERYONE JUST FORK A BLOCKCHAIN?

In theory everyone could, but it takes quite an effort. First, one has to generate enough demand for the new coins, otherwise they are worthless. And second, one has to solve the problem of the mining difficulty. Remember, the mining difficulty adjusts to a level, so that the entire network takes a certain time (for example 10 minutes in the case of Bitcoin) to find a new block (solve the puzzle). If the community splits in half, or in the example of Bitcoin (BTC) and Bitcoin Cash (BCH) in 2017 into 90% BTC and 10% BCH, based on statistics, it will take the BCH community 10x longer (100 minutes) to find a new block. This might not sound too bad at first, but it causes a lot of uncertainty, which is not good for the price of the new coin and, therefore, the interest of the community. While the electricity and equipment costs stay the same as before the fork, it is now not clear when and how often rewards are being paid for mining in return. BCH truly struggled with that during the first days and were it not for several political and economic reasons, BCH, just like 99% of all other fork attempts, would have probably not survived. Aside of the mining difficulty, so-called replay attacks may happen during a fork.

WHAT ARE REPLAY ATTACKS?

Replay Attacks occur when someone copies/replays a transaction from one chain to the other chain after the fork.

How is this possible? Very simple. Since you sign a transaction with your private key, which leads to a unique transaction ID (puzzle piece), a person merely has to go to the other chain, copy your ID (which is the same, since the chains are essentially a clone of each other up to the point when the fork happened), and replay the transaction. This can be avoided by installing a replay protection, which will make this no longer possible. Many forks do not implement that, which causes massive problems. This is exactly what happened during the first weeks of the Ethereum/Classic fork, and it took a few weeks until it was solved.

WHAT SHOULD YOU BE DOING DURING A FORK?

If you own a coin where a fork is happening, the only thing you can do is to NOT send your coins anywhere. You just wait it out, until a replay protection gets installed by the community, and the dust of chaos has settled.

Aside from more or less legit attempts to fork a chain, miners can run attacks on a chain.

WHAT ARE BLOCKCHAIN ATTACKS?

Blockchain attacks are not as relevant with large blockchains today since they are very difficult to achieve and get called out by the community right away. Speaking in game theoretical terms, there is a point in a blockchain where attacking it is way less profitable than being part of it. Game theory creates mathematical models of how intelligent and rational decision-makers would behave in certain scenarios.

> **IMPORTANT**
> The larger and the more distributed a blockchain community gets, the less likely it will get attacked.

In Bitcoin, it has become clear that the only "real attack" that is profitable is WITHHOLDING BLOCKS.

WHY WOULD MINERS WITHHOLD BLOCKS?

Withholding a block means that a miner who finds a block does not immediately broadcast it to the rest of the network, but keeps it to themselves. At first glance, this makes absolutely no sense. If a miner does not broadcast his newly found block, the rest of the community does not acknowledge that they earned the mining reward. So why would they do that? Since it takes 10 minutes on average to find a block, there are cases where someone finds a block a lot earlier, let's say three minutes. Mining is a probability game, not an actual math game. So, once they find this block out of sheer luck, the miner keeps it, while the rest of the community looks for a new valid block.

Let's say it takes them ten minutes to find it, and it gets broadcasted to the entire network. Initially one might think, that the miner who has found a block after only three minutes just lost out on the rewards because even if they broadcast the block now, it will get rejected by the network since it's too late. The miner takes a longer shot however, and attempts to also find the next block before everyone else. If the rest of the community takes another 10 minutes for that block, it will have taken them 20 minutes for both. This "malicious" miner now has around 16 minutes for the second block, which they will definitely need, because they will surely take longer than 10 minutes, as they are now mining alone. Now let's assume, they do find a new block in 16 minutes. They can now broadcast BOTH blocks to the network, and since both blocks are VALID and now constitute the LONGEST CHAIN, everyone drops the old block (which becomes an orphan block) and accepts the two new ones. The "malicious" miner is recognized as having received the mining rewards for BOTH blocks in a row, something that normally never occurs, and they will make a way larger reward. The miner thereby is not malicious in a way that tries to attack the network, like during a 51% attack or similar, but rather by cheating the system to get an even higher reward.

WHAT IS A 51% ATTACK?

In a 51% attack, over 51% of the mining power is colluded within one group, which is now controlling the entire consensus and can control transactions, censorship, and pretty much anything associated with the blockchain. A 51% attack would make a decentralized system centralized. It is highly hypothetical, as it would not only need over 51% of the mining power, but on top of that, none of the other 49% to notice. If people in the 49% started to notice, they would first of all complain about the centralization, followed by them selling their coins if it does not get resolved. Both actions would make the price drop significantly, and the people running the 51% attack would most likely not have a significant profit, if one at all.

Let's assume 51% of a blockchain community does manage to perform such an attack without the others noticing. What could this group do? First of all, they could start blocking transactions from and to certain people by simply not including their transactions into any blocks. Even if other miners picked them up, the 51% group always "out-mines" the rest, and their chain will stay the longest. Second, they could perform double spending attacks by sending the same coins in very short times apart to different people. Since they are in charge of creating consensus, they can game the rest. Thirdly, they could change the history if their power is significantly larger than 51%. Since they would have to mine every single block again, this would be quite a task and highly unlikely, but nevertheless, possible.

Overall, a 51% attack is highly improbable and most of the time not economical, even though it might appear to be at first glance. The last attack I will cover is called a sybil attack and is also highly theoretical.

WHAT IS A SYBIL ATTACK?

A sybil attack works by creating many other fake participants at very low or even no cost in order to sway the consensus algorithm to one's own interest.

The reason why creating consensus cannot be free is exactly because of this attack. Since all legit blockchains have a "cost" of participating in the consensus (mining), it is difficult to run such an attack, as one had to outperform the rest of the group, which is extremely costly. Again, the more people participate in a blockchain, the more stable it becomes, and that is why sybil attacks are very theoretical today. So, if all these attacks and hacks are not that relevant, what could destroy a blockchain?

CHAPTER 8 – DESTROYING
A BLOCKCHAIN

Let's discuss a few potential culprits that could destroy a blockchain and also how they would play out.

QUANTUM COMPUTING

A blockchain is backed by cryptography, and if the trust in that cryptography fails, so does the backing. People call this "hacking a blockchain." Remember, whenever we hear today about a blockchain being hacked, what the press actually means is that a private key or database with keys was hacked, not the blockchain itself. One objection from "blockchain-antagonists" is the possibility of quantum computers being able to back-calculate the algorithms, thereby making private keys known and any protection redundant. This would truly mean that a blockchain was hacked. While this is true in theory, in reality there are already quantum computer resistant cryptographies being used, which could further be implemented into other blockchains such as Bitcoin or Ethereum, even though they are not using them right now. So, in case a computer could "break the code," there would be a sharp dip initially, followed by an adjustment of the protocol and the blockchain's recovery. A true "hack" of a blockchain does NOT really seem possible that way.

REGULATION / PROHIBITION

The second danger that always pops up when talking about crypto-currencies is that of regulation or even prohibition by a large country or government. The argument makes sense. Since decentralized cryptocurrencies pose a danger to the centralized currencies of such legislations, banks and regulators should have an interest to keep cryptocurrencies suppressed. There is a big flaw in that logic though: Governments LOVE cryptocurrencies…as long as they can control them. Why? Think about what a blockchain as a transparent ledger allows any government to do; if you know who the account holders are, with the click of a button, you can track all incomes, expenses, taxes, etc. Government paradise! I know for a fact that many central banks are looking into this for exactly that reason. They want to create cryptocurrencies where only they have such insight, and they can "sell" it to people as an advancement of the current fiat system. Personally, I am not against them doing it, as long as people know the difference between a public cryptocurrency such as Bitcoin and a controlled one, as one created by a country.

So why don't countries stop the public cryptocurrencies? Countries understand that something that is digital, open source and decentralized cannot really be stopped. How would you go about it? Bitcoin, for example, is NOT a company. There is nothing to shut down. Illegalize cryptocurrency apps? They are open source, which means that is not really possible. Illegalize companies? That would only work for exchanges, but even those are starting to become decentralized. Illegalize owning cryptocurrencies or mining? How would someone be able to check? If a country truly tried to block public blockchains, what they would end up with is a bad reputation for their own private blockchain and a lot of illegal use of the public blockchains by those that don't care about the law. Not a desirable outcome. But there might be a final blow-out punch; blockchains need their participants to communicate, so why not try the last blockchain attack: Shutting down the internet.

SHUT DOWN OF THE INTERNET

Without the internet, people could not keep up a decentralized ledger, so, one big danger for blockchains is for a government to shut off or regulate the internet, right? Wrong! Aside from the fact that it is quite impossible to shut down the internet, consider how many applications that are absolutely essential for everyday life use the internet. Even if the government managed to shut it down, so-called mesh-networks would appear instantly. Mesh-networks are true peer-to-peer networks, where people send information to each other via other people, rather than through servers and routers. Think about it: the internet is nothing other than a network for information. Shutting it down would mean to remove the routers and servers, but actually one would not need them if people just transferred the information directly. During protests, many countries try to suppress the protests by taking away the people's internet access. People just connect to each other via Bluetooth and direct wireless connections, and within days, full text messaging functionalities are restored. Taking this a step further, to ensure the independence and sustainability of Bitcoin, a core group is actually thinking about sending special satellites into space. Shutting down the internet to bring down a blockchain is therefore not really feasible.

One objection by critics of blockchains that gets raised a lot was also one of the first email replies Satoshi got to his Bitcoin whitepaper in 2008: "The storage of all the data from a blockchain must consume incredible amounts of disk space—how should this scale going forward if everyone has to keep a record of everything that has been happening?"

BLOCKCHAIN SIZE

We handled that objection already in the mining chapter, but let's pick it up again and look into it in detail. At the moment, in 2017, the Bitcoin blockchain alone is close to 200 gigabytes large, adding 1 megabyte every 10 minutes. Ethereum is even larger and growing faster. So, what is there to counter argue, other than we have simple payment verification? Someone has to store all this data… How should this be sustainable?

First of all, transaction speeds and storage possibilities will keep going up exponentially. Twenty years ago, a floppy disk merely had 1MB of space. 10 years ago, we started calculating in gigabytes, and today most disks have terabytes of space. These are all improvements of 1,000x within 10 years each. If you look at the speed of the internet, you can see a similar pattern: 20 years ago, a 64K modem being able to do a few kilobytes a second was considered great. 10 years ago, with the appearance of broadband, streaming with a few megabytes became possible. Today, we can already transact at close to 1 gigabyte speeds, which is the same 1,000x improvement as storing capabilities. If capacities and speed keep growing even just at a fraction of that rate, which continues to happen routinely, we will not run into any significant blockchain-size problems anytime soon. It is simply exponential space and speed technology keeping up with linear growth of a blockchain.

Additionally, we have seen other possibilities emerge about how all the data could be stored. Some forms use a more "regional" approach, where nodes only keep the information of the "neighbors" and not the entire blockchain. Some systems rely on a peer-to-peer model on top of existing blockchains. All these solutions would reduce the need for everyone to store all the data and therefore reduce the problems associated with blockchain size and growth.

So if none of the aforementioned things could kill a blockchain, what could? The answer might surprise you. It is the same thing that created the need for a blockchain in the first place: a centralized system.

CENTRALIZATION

We turn toward blockchain technologies because we don't trust a centralized system, but on the other hand, if there was indeed full trust into such a centralized system, there would be no need for blockchains, including their applications such as cryptocurrencies. A decentralized system comes with cost, speed, lack of being in charge, and so on—all things that we are willing to compromise for, as it allows the community to be in control.

What could kill a blockchain is the full trust of a community in a centralized power.

But how likely is it to have a benevolent dictator who is in control and still receives all the trust? Personally, I do not see anyone or anything creating such trust in the near future, so I am convinced that blockchains and their applications are here to stay. However, I also do NOT belong to the group of people who believe that decentralization is the only way forward. I believe in having a choice and not being forced into having to use something. The reason I love blockchains, decentralization, and cryptocurrencies is that they give me that choice. Probably some centralized organizations will recognize that and will understand that they have to give in if they want to survive. That is what it will come down to eventually: centralized organizations offering decentralized services, thereby providing their users the best out of both worlds.

Decentralization is the urgently needed checks and balances to centralization.

We have already thrown around some terms such as privacy, anonymity, and transparency, and in the next chapter, we will look at what they actually mean and how private cryptocurrencies really are.

CHAPTER 9 – PRIVACY,
ANONYMITY AND TRANSPARENCY

You might have heard or read that cryptocurrencies are a great way to launder money, do illegal things, and avoid taxes because they are so private and no one knows what is actually happening under the hood. Let's look at how true this statement actually is. To do that, we need to understand some basic terminologies first.

WHAT IS PRIVACY?

Privacy is the ability of an individual or group to seclude themselves, or information about themselves, and thereby express themselves selectively (https://en.wikipedia.org/wiki/Anonymity). When it comes to money, two components of privacy are especially important: **Anonymity** and **Transparency**. Privacy is a function that looks like this:

$$P = A / T$$

Privacy is the highest when Anonymity is at its highest and Transparency is at its lowest.

WHAT IS ANONYMITY?

Anonymity, or the adjective "anonymous," is derived from the Greek word ἀνωνυμία, anonymia meaning "without a name" or "namelessness" (https://en.wikipedia.org/wiki/Anonymity). In the case of money, this means that no one knows who hides behind an account number. Since a blockchain does not distinguish between age, race, country, gender, or background, it seems as if there is 100% anonymity in cryptocurrencies regarding who or what generated a private key by random.

WHAT IS KYC, KYB, AML AND CTF?

Not knowing who is who would be a regulatory nightmare for a government. That's why central authorities do anti-money-laundering (AML), counter financing terrorism (CFT), and know your customer or business (KYC or KYB) checks. In the case of cryptocurrencies, exchanges have to do these checks.

Only based on anonymity, privacy would be 100%, since it is very easy to seclude information about who you send money to or receive it from, as long as you stay away from exchanges. However, there is a second component to privacy that changes everything: transparency.

WHAT IS TRANSPARENCY?

Transparency, not in the definition of light being able to shine through something, but rather as used in business, the humanities, and in other social contexts implies openness, communication, and accountability. Transparency is operating in such a way that it is easy for others to see what actions are performed. What this means is that the pathways of how money flows are known—and that is where most blockchains are 100% transparent, even over its entire history. There are some newer technologies, which we will discuss in a later chapter, like zero-knowledge-proofs and ring-signatures, that would bring transparency down and thereby privacy up, but their use is still very limited.

WHAT DOES PSEUDO-ANONYMOUS MEAN?

In a blockchain, anonymity (who is the owner) might be very low, however transparency (what happened) is very high. Since this creates an interesting effect on privacy, people call cryptocurrencies pseudo-anonymous. A computer could back-calculate the 100% transparent transactions and put the pieces together until anonymity might not be 0% but maybe 1%. That could be enough to identify who committed a certain financial crime or not.

ARE CRYPTOCURRENCIES HANDY FOR ILLEGAL ACTIVITIES?

People believe that cryptocurrencies are great for illegal activities, as they believe Bitcoin for example is so private. The highest form of privacy possible, however, is cash; no one knows who owns it and who it is given to. That is why governments want to get rid of it. Imagine what this would mean for tax evasion and other crimes. Literally with the press of a button, the revenue department would know all your spending and revenue or law enforcement could instantly see any money laundering or illegal purchases.

It was this exactly that was shown in the case of Ross Ulbricht, who was imprisoned to a life sentence in 2015 for money laundering and drug trafficking with cryptocurrencies (https://en.wikipedia.org/wiki/Ross_Ulbricht). This crime was only connected to him through the combination of bringing anonymity up a slight bit and having 100% access to the entire transaction history. This helped to figure out his identity and showed once again that cryptocurrencies are NOT suited for illegal activities.

WHAT IS INTIMACY AND SECRECY?

There is one important personal input that I would like to make here: While I am completely against committing any crimes, I am for a certain amount of intimacy (a level of privacy that most people want to have in their lives) that any individual is entitled to in my opinion. People should be able to pay at a hospital, for example, without the entire rest of the world knowing what their ailment was. Obviously, there is a fine line, when such intimacy exaggerates into "secrecy" (a certain amount of transparency, many times associated with malicious behavior), and that is what makes this topic about privacy so sensitive. If you are freaked out by cryptocurrencies creating a "Big Brother," don't worry—there are solutions to that, which you will discover in the next chapter.

CHAPTER 10 – ALTCOINS AND BITCOIN

WHAT ARE ALTCOINS?

Altcoins are historically defined as any ryptocurrency other than Bitcoin.

Altcoins (=alternative coins) are simply other blockchains with a new set of rules that the participating community has agreed on. It is important that whenever you hear about a new coin or blockchain, which pop up like weeds in a garden, you check first to determine if it is legit or not. You can find a list of most legit cryptocurrencies on www.coinmarketcap.com. Additionally, I still urge you to do your own due diligence.

HOW TO RECOGNIZE SCAMS

There is no fixed map in order to decide what is a scam and what is legit, but I will try to give you a compass with seven points:

1. If a cryptocurrency **promises guaranteed** returns that are significantly higher than traditional investments, such as real estate or stocks (5-7% per year), be careful for it might be a scam. No one can promise guaranteed returns higher than a few percent a year. They are possible, but definitely not guaranteed.

2. If a cryptocurrency is **private**, meaning it is not open source and does not have a public blockchain with a transaction ledger, it might be a scam.

3. If a cryptocurrency is **mainly pre-mined** and the owner holds the majority of the currency, it might be a scam. There are a few exceptions, but in general, you should be careful if the creator of a currency owns most of his/her own currency, which would allow him/her to fully control the price.

4. If a cryptocurrency has a network marketing model attached to it and is advertised to you as an **"opportunity,"** it is most likely a scam. There are many cryptocurrency companies who have a legit affiliate system, where you get 5-10% from any customer you refer to them, but if you see companies or cryptocurrencies that focus more on recruiting than actually delivering a product or service, beware.

5. **Cloud mining opportunities** in combination with a referral scheme are most likely scams. The detailed reasons for this are laid out in the mining chapter, but in summary, this has to do with the very thin margins and tough competition. Mostly, these companies do not pay out mining profits, but forward the investments of other people in a Ponzi type scheme.

6. If a cryptocurrency pops up that does **not really create value,** but is just there to exist, it might be a scam. Sadly, this applies to most cryptocurrencies, and while some of them have an increasing price right now, they will blow up sooner or later.

7. Just like with cryptocurrencies, **most so-called Initial Coin Offerings (ICOs)** are also scams. Most companies doing an ICO are startups with no team, no product and no customers. Be extra careful when investing into an ICO.

There are always exceptions to these seven points, and you can surely make a quick buck investing into scams, but from a moral and economic standpoint, I must urge you to do your due diligence and stay away from them. "If it smells fishy and looks fishy...it's a fish!" The funny thing is, if you apply these rules to fiat currencies like EUR, USD, etc. you will find that they all fall under the "scam" category. The only reason they don't get accused of being one is because we trust the issuing agency—whether we should or not is definitely up for debate.

WHAT ARE LEGITIMATE RESOURCES FOR INFORMATION?

Having a good source for legitimate information is essential in an eco-system that is as rapidly developing as cryptocurrencies. The challenge is that there are more bad resources out there than good ones. Therefore, one has to be very selective. Here is a list I can recommend:

Official Reddit threads:
https://www.reddit.com/r/Bitcoin/
https://www.reddit.com/r/ethereum/
https://www.reddit.com/r/ethtrader/
https://www.reddit.com/r/cryptocurrencies

YouTube Channels:
https://www.youtube.com/julianhospenglish

Magazines:
https://bitcoinmagazine.com/
https://cointelegraph.com/
https://www.coindesk.com/

Facebook Groups:
www.facebook.com/groups/cryptofit

Lists & overviews:
http://www.coinmarketcap.com
https://www.smithandcrown.com/icos/

Whenever you stumble across a new resource, always ask yourself, "What are the economic incentives for the person or company who is providing the info?" Then remember, no one will cut off the hand that feeds him or her. A great tip is to look for a group you can update yourself and give each other legit tips. Google "Julian Hosp Crypto Mastermind" if you want to look at what we have created for our community. This was one of the most breakthrough things I have done for myself, and it has given me over 100x returns for some of my crypto investments.

WHICH CRYPTOCURRENCIES ARE WORTH LOOKING INTO?

Let me give you an overview of some of the cryptocurrencies that I personally do consider as interesting.

WARNING: Please understand that I might be completely wrong in my personal perception. These mentions are in no way to be seen as investment advice or an endorsement! Always do your own due diligence when investing your hard-earned money, and understand that this list was created end of 2017—by the time you are reading this, things can be upside down.

BITCOIN (CORE) BTC

We have spoken about Bitcoin in great detail already, and I have written a whole lot about it; simply search for "Julian Hosp Bitcoin," if you want all the details on the "mother of all cryptocurrencies," also called "digital gold." Since Bitcoin was forked several times, I am talking about the main chain, which is also called Bitcoin Core. After it was defined in 2008 by Satoshi Nakamoto, its first block was mined on January 3rd, 2009. The first-ever Bitcoin transaction to another person happened nine days later on January 12th, 2009, when Satoshi sent 10 bitcoins, back then worth nothing—today worth a hundred thousand dollars—to a gentleman called Hal Finney. The first ever recorded purchase with bitcoins was that of "Laszlo" on May 22nd, 2010. He bought a pizza worth 25 USD for 10,000 bitcoins. In 2017, this would have been worth close to 100 million USD.

I personally learned about Bitcoin in 2011, just when it hit 1 USD. I did not see the potential though and considered it to be a scam. Bitcoin shot up to over 1,000 USD in 2013, just before the largest exchange back then, called MtGox, announced it got hacked, and the price plummeted to 200 USD over the following years. I bought my first bitcoin in 2014 at 800 USD, panicked when it hit 400 USD a few months later and then bought again at 500 USD. Since then, I have kept buying in regular periods. Since 2015 Bitcoin has seen an ever-increasing popularity with its price climbing higher and higher. Bitcoin uses a proof-of-work algorithm, where a reward is given to the miner who finds a new block. Originally that was 50 bitcoins every block, but is halved every 210,000 blocks, or approximately every 4 years. The first halving from 50 to 25 bitcoins happened on November 28th, 2012, and the latest halving from 25 to 12.5 bitcoins took place on July 9th, 2016. The next halving from 12.5 to 6.25 bitcoins per block is expected to happen around the beginning of June 2020. This halving will occur 64 times until the reward hits 1 Satoshi per block sometime in a hundred years or so. After that, it cannot be halved anymore, and the total number of bitcoins will remain close to 21 million (just slightly below). Since the supply of new bitcoins is exponentially decreasing, there are already close to 17 million bitcoins in circulation, even though only nine years have passed.

Bitcoin has focused heavily on stability rather than innovation, which has provided its fair share of criticism. There are regular BIPs (Bitcoin Improvement Proposals), but any that take an extreme approach to change something radically get rejected by the community quite rapidly. This makes it hard to try out new concepts, but Bitcoin wants to stand its ground for being "digital gold." When all crypto-hell breaks loose, Bitcoin wants to be here to stay. It has the largest community, the widest acceptance, the greatest market capitalization, and the lowest volatility. Also, as mentioned earlier already, a core group is now even planning to send Bitcoin satellites into space to provide internet specifically for Bitcoin, in case governments should ever start to close down on cryptocurrencies.

WHO IS SATOSHI NAKAMOTO, AND HOW MANY BITCOINS DOES HE OWN?

No one knows who he is, and the wildest theories have been thrown around, ranking from him being from Japan to actually being the NSA themselves. Most people agree that it was most likely a group of people that used that name as a pseudonym, as some of the code and texts appear as if they were written by different individuals. A few people have been suspected or even claimed being Satoshi, but all of these assumptions were dismissed.

It would be very easy for someone to prove that he/she/they is/are

Satoshi. During the first days or maybe even weeks, it can be assumed that it was only Satoshi who did any of the mining. There simply was no one else. Calculations have revealed that Satoshi must own 1-2 million bitcoins, which are spread over different wallets and worth several billion USD. Satoshi would only have to sign any of these bitcoins with his private key, confirming it is truly him/her/them. These bitcoins are being watched very carefully by the entire Bitcoin community. If they ever moved, "Bitcoin-hell" would break loose. From a creator's view, it is quite difficult for Satoshi to ever cash in on his/her/their fortune since it is expected that the price would plummet in such a scenario. However, most people expect that he/she/they don't have the private keys anymore anyways and the access to these bitcoins is lost. Such an assumption is not too far-fetched, considering that at the beginning of 2009, 1 bitcoin would have been worth literally nothing. Would you have written down all the different private keys and stored them safely for something worth nothing while you were probably just trying out some new stuff without expecting it to ever take off? Maybe, but probably not. In Satoshi's case, we might never know.

ANY BITCOIN PRICE PREDICTION

Any types of predictions are hard, especially about the future. Therefore, rather than making a prediction, let me explain where some of the current price predictions of 500,000 to 1,000,000 USD that you might read about in the press are coming from. If we compare Bitcoin to gold and assume Bitcoin will therefore reach a similar market capitalization as gold has today, then the cap of Bitcoin would reach around 7 trillion USD at some point. At the end of 2017, Bitcoin has around 2% of that. Therefore, a price of 50x of what Bitcoin has today (around 10,000 USD per bitcoin) is possible, which would get 1 bitcoin close to half a million USD. However, there is one additional factor: lost private keys. One can assume that access to around 1/4 or maybe even 1/2 of all bitcoins is already lost or will be at some point. That would put the value of 1 bitcoin in the range of 0.5–1 million USD. At the rate bitcoin has been growing over the past years, it could hit that valuation within 7-10 years. Whether it will or will not, no one knows until then. So definitely do NOT take this paragraph as investment advice.

WHAT ARE FORKS OF BITCOIN (NAMECOIN, LITECOIN, BITCOIN CASH, . . .)?

As already talked about in the chapter about forks, people tried to create their own versions of a cryptocurrency. Instead of writing the entire code all over, one could just fork Bitcoin.

NAMECOIN NMC

Namecoin was the first Bitcoin fork and was introduced on April 18th, 2011, around two years after Bitcoin's creation. It had pretty much everything the same as Bitcoin, with the exception of being able to store data within its own blockchain transaction database. It was supposed to create the censorship-resistant domain.bit, which is functionally close to .com or other domains, but it would work independent of ICANN, which is the main and centralized governing body for domain names. After a promising start, Namecoin can be called a failure today, due to the cryptographic similarities to Bitcoin, which allowed miners to attack the fork, as we discussed in great detail in the forking chapter.

LITECOIN LTC

Learning from Namecoin's struggles, Charlie Lee, a former Google employee, forked Litecoin off of the Bitcoin code in October 2011 (6 months after Namecoin). He introduced Scrypt as a new proof of work algorithm, adjusted the mining difficulty to 2.5 minutes per block, and increased the total coin supply to 84 million litecoins (4x as much as Bitcoin). Litecoin is seen as Bitcoin's little brother, just like silver to gold. From a leadership perspective, Litecoin is definitely more centralized, as Charlie Lee is very active in pushing and promoting philosophies through the Litecoin community. This helps with innovation but also gets criticized by those who rather see a cryptocurrency be more decentralized. Litecoin was the first top-5 cryptocurrency based on market capitalization to adopt Segregated Witness (SegWit) in May 2017, and then also adopted the Lightning Network shortly after. Depending on its innovation, Litecoin could definitely keep its place among the top cryptocurrencies.

BITCOIN CASH / BCASH BCH

Bitcoin-Cash was the result of a fork on August 1st, 2017 when Bitcoin (Core) underwent its SegWit update, and the community around BCH did not. BCH has blocks of up to 8MB, allowing for 8x more transactions per block than BTC. BCH did not adopt SegWit, which was the main reason for its split off since SegWit requires slightly different mining hardware than BCH. Everything else is pretty similar between the two forks, and despite some massive pumps followed by dumps, BCH managed to stay among the top-10 cryptocurrencies. Whether it will keep its position or not is yet to be seen.

There are several other forks, which I will not focus on due to their minor importance If you google for a "complete bitcoin fork list" you will find 100s of other, mostly unsuccessful, forks. I will cover the two BTC forks DASH and ZCASH a bit later, when talking about private coins.

ETHEREUM ETH

If you consider Bitcoin to be a 1st generation blockchain, Ethereum deserves to be called a 2nd generation blockchain, where way more functions are possible. Ethereum was proposed by "child prodigy" Vitalik Buterin in late 2013, who suggested that instead of using a blockchain only for currencies, one could expand its functionalities into acting more like a decentralized computer. Instead of storing how many coins each participant has, this Ethereum computer, also called Ethereum Virtual Machine (EVM) would execute actual code. In order to fund the development, the Ethereum Foundation did an ICO crowdsale in the summer of 2014, where, depending on the time one participated, 1 BTC could get the buyer between 1,337–2,000 ETH. In total, they received a little bit over 31,529 BTC, which represented the desired 15 million USD at the time, putting the initial Ethereum price at around 30 cents. The system went live around a year later on July 30th, 2015.

WHAT ARE SMART CONTRACTS?

The biggest advancement to Bitcoin's blockchain is that Ethereum is using the so-called Turing-complete scripting language Solidity, which allows performing actual computations within the blockchain. While Bitcoin allows for basic multi-signature features, where two or more participants have to sign a transaction for it to be executed, Ethereum opened the opportunity for so-called smart contracts.

Smart Contracts are contracts where a
decentralized blockchain ensures its immutability and execution.

WHAT IS THE EVM (ETHEREUM VIRTUAL MACHINE)?

Just like any other computer, Ethereum has an operating system, which is called the EVM (Ethereum Virtual Machine). The EVM executes code that is stored on all the participating nodes throughout the network. If you have a program that you never want to be able to be stopped by an outside force, Ethereum can run it for you completely decentralized and the initiator of the program needs to pay "gas." This is paid in Ethereum's currency, Ether, and is similar to how you have to pay Amazon in order to run a server on their cloud service or how you have transaction fees in Bitcoin. The EVM started with version 0, called Olympic, in May 2015. Then, it upgraded to version 1, Frontier, in July 2015 and version 2, Homestead, in March 2016. It is currently running version 3, Metropolis, sub-version Byzantium, where it added so-called zero-knowledge-snarks, which allow you to break the transparency of a blockchain, while still being cryptographically secure. An interesting upgrade will be the next version, 3.5 Metropolis-Constantinople, as it will make Ethereum switch to a Proof-of-Stake from its current Proof-of-Work consensus algorithm. Ethereum is one of the most forward-pushing blockchain technologies out there, trying to innovate as often as possible, which is in big contrast to Bitcoin, where developers are more focused on risk avoidance rather than innovation.

ANY PRICE PREDICTION ON ETHEREUM?

Just like in Bitcoin, any price predictions of Ethereum is quite difficult, so do NOT take this as investment advice. If you compare Ethereum and other platforms to centralized operating systems such as OS, Windows, and Linux, one can imagine that a few of the decentralized platforms will also survive. Microsoft's market cap is close to 600 billion USD, and considering the more diverse applications Ethereum could offer, a total market cap of a few trillion USD, just like Bitcoin, is imaginable, which would put 1 ETH at 30,000 USD. Obviously, no one knows, and this is pure guessing! Some people even claim ETH could go higher than Bitcoin… Only the future knows.

HOW DID ETHEREUM CLASSIC GET CREATED?

Different to Bitcoin, where the person of Satoshi is unknown, Ethereum has its lead figure in Vitalik Buterin, which gives it, similar to Litecoin, its fair amount of criticism of not being as decentralized as a blockchain should be. For example, in the summer of 2016 an investment vehicle called the DAO (Decentralized Autonomous Organization) was conceived. Around 150 million USD worth of ETH was invested, only to find out that a hacker managed to steal almost half of the money. Breaking the "code is law" credo, the Ethereum Foundation around Vitalik "undid" the damage, by forking the Ethereum blockchain, as if the DAO never happened. The mutated fork was still called Ethereum, and the old unaltered version received the name **Ethereum Classic ETC**. As one can imagine, this caused a big uproar in the entire crypto-community, since it led to the question of how decentralized Ethereum and how immutable a blockchain truly was. From a price perspective however, Ethereum Classic is currently lacking the developer power needed to compete against its larger brother, Ethereum

ETH and therefore most of the attention is on the altered version.

WHAT ARE ERC20 TOKENS?

While many exciting applications that could run on the EVM have been envisioned, the main use for Ethereum's technology in 2016 and 2017 was that of companies not having to create their own blockchain, but rather creating their own tokens through a smart contract on Ethereum. These so-called ERC20 tokens (Ethereum Request for Comments Nr. 20) define six very easy functions: 1) total token amount, 2) how many tokens anyone has, 3) where to transfer tokens from and 4) to whom, 5) whether something gets approved or not, 6) and if a certain feature is allowed or not. Instead of companies having to invest into their own blockchain with miners, servers, etc., it now takes half an afternoon to create their own "currencies." It simply relies on Ethereum's infrastructure. The main function for these ERC20 tokens is that of ICOs: Initial Coin Offerings.

WHAT IS AN ICO?

In an ICO, a company sells part or all of a newly pre-mined token in return for receiving other cryptocurrencies, just like Ethereum did for their own start. They do serve a valuable purpose, as long as they are structured in a legit and not scammy way. I have written entire blog posts and article on this, so simply google "Julian Hosp ICO." Also, check the bonus chapter at the end of the book about this topic. Let me introduce some of the more popular tokens. You can see a full list on www.coinmarketcap.com.

ERC20 TOKEN OVERVIEW (REP, ICN, MLN, DGD, ETC.)

- Augur REP: a betting token that allows you to bet on anything in the Augur system.
- Iconomi ICN & Melonport MLN: a token that you use to invest into other cryptocurrencies like using an ETF.
- DigiX DGD: a gold token that allows you to benefit from gold.

Even though I am mentioning them, I do not know how these tokens play out in the future, so do NOT see this as investment advice. Most of these tokens can be bought on www.bittrex.com.

OTHER "DECENTRALIZED PLATFORMS" (NEM, LISK, WAVES, STRATIS, ETC.…)

Aside of Ethereum and Ethereum Classic, several other decentralized computing platforms have started to emerge. Most of these systems promise easier and better technologies, for example by not using Ethereum's programming language Solidity, which no one outside of Ethereum actually uses, as it is considered quite difficult and buggy. While many of these newer platforms appear fruitful, as of writing this book at the end of 2017, none of them have received the traction and attention that Ethereum has. This is a crucial step, considering that the internet is not using the best technology possible, but it has gained the most traction and is therefore used worldwide.

OTHER APPLICATION- OR BACKED-BY-SOMETHING-TOKENS

Companies not wanting to use an Ethereum-based token can either use any of the other platforms (even Bitcoin is possible as a so-called color coin) or create their own blockchain. Steem, for example, is trying to build a decentralized social media system of people creating valuable content get paid in Steem Dollars.

WHAT IS TOKENIZATION?

Tokenization means that real-world-assets like stocks, bonds, real estate, gold, etc. are being brought onto the blockchain.

While I am a big fan of tokenization and I believe it is definitely the future, one has to be very cautious about whether the underlying assets exist or not, especially with Tether USDT, which I have my personal reservations about. I am not sure how many actual dollars are in Bitfinex's vault, who created this currency. However, it will be very exciting to see all the new possibilities coming up in the next years with more and more companies and real-world assets being represented on the blockchain.

PRIVATE COINS (MONERO, DASH, ZCASH, ETC.)

Considering the high transparency traditional blockchains have (everyone can see which address sends coins to what other address), several new systems have been suggested to increase privacy. A phenomenon that could occur otherwise is that of non-fungibility. A good currency needs to have the three functionalities unit of account, method to transfer, and store of value. The unit of account in particular only works if one coin is the same as another. In a fully transparent decentralized system, this feature can struggle, since coins can become "tainted."

WHAT ARE TAINTED COINS?

Tainted coins are coins where one can connect their use to illegal activities in their past and therefore become less valuable than non-tainted coins.

For example, bitcoins might get stolen from someone. The thief then sends these bitcoins to an exchange, and before the exchanges can do anything, he changes them to Ether and withdraws those immediately. The bitcoins are now tainted because they are associated with illegal activities. No one wants to receive these tainted bitcoins, since everyone knows they actually belong to the person they were stolen from. In the fiat world, this is not possible, as money on a bank account is not numbered, and bank notes do not track their history.

The solution in the crypto world is to put these tainted coins into a "mixer," where they get mixed with enough non-tainted coins and instead of a single coin being completely tainted, all coins get tainted by a few percent. For example, imagine there is 1 tainted bitcoin. If it gets mixed with 99 non-tainted coins, every one of the 100 bitcoins is now 1% tainted. Through this method, pretty much most bitcoins today are tainted to a certain degree, which is not a real problem – yet. Some exchanges have actually started to track the "taintedness" of coins, and if you tried to deposit a coin that was tainted too much, they would reject your deposit. While this rarely happens, people do think about how to solve this problem. This is why more private coins, in which their history is not fully known, were created. How do they work? While more methods are being developed, there are mainly three technologies in use right now:

RING SIGNATURES (MONERO XMR)

Ring signatures work in a way where instead of one person signing a transaction (puzzle piece), they sign all the other transactions (puzzle pieces) that happen within a block as well. All the other people sending something within that same block do the same, so transactions get signed by a ring of people. To an outside observer looking at the blockchain, it becomes quite hard to track who sent coins to whom. He can only verify that the total number of coins that were sent and received by all participants are correct, but everyone is signing a bit of everything, not who received how much. The downside of this solution is that it can be possible that only a few people participate during such a ring signature procedure, which would increase the transparency and thereby decrease privacy. The upside is that it takes no one else, other than the people participating in the block of the transactions, to verify them.

MIXERS (DASH ...)

Mixers work in a way where other people that are NOT part of the transaction provide large pools of coins. These pools are called mixers, which are being used to mix coins that are sent by others. In the case of DASH, master-nodes provide such pools, and in return for them "staking" their coins, they get incentivized by the community. These are the two major downsides of this method to increase privacy: you need other people for it to work and it will incur some kind of cost. The upside compared to ring signatures is that even if you do a transaction all by yourself, you still have maximum privacy. Imagine mixers like a huge swimming pool (the coins in the mixer) that you pour a glass of water (the coins you want to send) into. You then tell the person you want to send coins to how much water (how many coins) he is allowed to take out of the pool. Since this communication of "how much" does not get recorded on the blockchain, it is not traceable afterwards. In this case, it is impossible to ever track the coins, since no one knows afterwards who took whose water out of the pool. In the case of ring signatures, the pool is formed by the people making the transactions. It does not require others, but if the created pool (ring signature) is too small, the water (coins) becomes traceable.

ZERO KNOWLEDGE PROOFS: (ZCASH, ETHEREUM,....)

Zero-knowledge proofs are the most powerful way for increased privacy, as they neither require anyone else, nor do they incur any fees. Traditional blockchain cryptography works in a way where you sign a transaction with your private key. No one can calculate what your private key looks like, but by seeing the puzzle piece, they can easily confirm that you own the private key. The puzzle piece is the trace that tells everyone who is sending coins to whom, which puts trust into the blockchain. Zero-knowledge proofs take the cryptography a step further and do what the name suggests: They allow someone to prove that they own the private key without showing others what the puzzle piece looks like. Therefore, they can send money to someone else without leaving a trace.

How this works in cryptography is quite a complex process, and you can google a detailed description by searching for "Julian Hosp zero-knowledge proofs." To put it into simple terms, imagine it like typing the PIN code into a phone. The pin code resembles the private key. For someone to prove that they know the PIN code of the phone, all they have to do is to unlock the phone and display the unlocked screen. This would resemble the puzzle piece in the blockchain. If you can see the screen, they must know the private key. Now imagine they would want to prove that they own the private key, but they don't want anyone to see the puzzle piece. Basically, they don't want anyone to see the unlocked phone, but they do want to prove that they can unlock the phone with the PIN. Obviously, they cannot reveal the PIN, otherwise everyone would know the private key and control the coins. So, what could they do instead? They could log in to the phone, not allow anyone to look at it, but instead activate a wireless hotspot. Others can now check whether they were indeed able to log in. If the hotspot is visible, they must have been able to log in and therefore known the PIN without anyone ever seeing the phone. With zero-knowledge-proofs the concept is similar: People sign a transaction without revealing the final result, but instead reveal a clue that proves based on probability that they were able to sign properly. This allows transactions without revealing the amount nor the recipient.

This would be by far the best cryptographic solution, as it does not need other people and it is incredibly efficient. There is just one major downside: The cryptographic function requires a so-called master key. Whoever knows this key can sign any transaction and can control the entire blockchain. Imagine it like a governmental agency knowing a master key, which they could use to unlock any phone. They will always know the right PIN, but no one would know whether it was the actual PIN that was specific to that phone or the master key. In the creation of ZCash for example, this master key was created by a group of people, who then displayed on camera how they all destroyed it. Several times, doubts arose on whether they truly destroyed the key or not, and several investigations have been launched. Even though it appears to be legit, this weakness is the make or break of this technology. Improvements to the cryptography are being worked on, and many other cryptocurrencies are looking into adding some of this extra privacy to their own blockchain. Ethereum for example, added so-called zk-snarks (zero-knowledge-snarks) with their Byzantium update in October 2017, and others are expected to follow in the future.

IS THIS PRIVACY GOOD OR BAD?

One big scrutiny all these private cryptocurrencies are facing is the following question: What would a currency be used for that is not traceable at all and knows no boundaries? Immediate answers would be drugs, prostitution, money laundering, etc. While some of the criticism might be rectified, one needs not only to keep the problem of fungibility in consideration, but furthermore should ask whether they would want for anyone to know that they were just hospitalized, that they are spending their holidays somewhere, or what they just invested in? So, while lots of privacy has its pros and cons, the magic will be somewhere in the middle. Some anonymity and some transparency are not only okay, but needed, and that is why these private coins definitely have a place in the crypto ecosystem.

BANKING COINS (RIPPLE, STELLAR LUMEN, R3, ETC....)

If you believe that banks are against cryptocurrencies, you are absolutely wrong. Many banks and countries are actually working on their own solutions, and some have even started to test collaborations. These banking coin solutions, just like Ripple XRP, Stellar Lumen XLM, R3, and many others, focus on speed and scalability. The most popular one, Ripple, receives most of its criticism from the blockchain community as the creators kept 100% of the tokens and sold them off piece by piece, still keeping the majority today. So, while Ripple has some interesting applications, this centralized ownership is a big red flag, and one has to see how this will turn out in the future. If you want to see some more details on Ripple, simply Google: "Julian Hosp Ripple." XLM is a fork of Ripple because of that reason. R3 in combination with Corda focuses more on building a network of banks. Out of this group, I personally own Ripple, which is NOT an investment advice.

NON-BLOCKCHAIN SOLUTIONS IOTA TANGLE & HASHGRAPH

The main target of non-blockchain solutions is that of solving scalability. In a blockchain, the speed and processing power of one node is the limit for the entire blockchain. If that node cannot process more than 100 transactions per second, it is the maximum capacity of the entire network since the node needs to keep a record of everything that is happening.

IOTA solves this by creating a so-called **tangle**. Instead of having to know everything, nodes only store the data of their neighbors and trust others to do so, as well, when enough confirmations have happened. These confirmations happen by anyone having to confirm (checking the validity of) other transactions before one can send a transaction themselves. Thereby, the concept of IOTA looks very promising to solve scalability, but it raises several questions on whether such a system could be attacked, cheated, and eventually actually be used.

The **hashgraph** is building on top of that concept and uses **"gossip about gossip"** as a protocol to spread consensus.

At this moment, products like IOTA and the hashgraph are more in a Proof-of-Concept than actual use stage. If you want more details on it, simply Google "Julian Hosp IOTA" and "Julian Hosp hashgraph".

BLOCKCHAIN CONNECTORS (LIGHTNING, RAIDEN, INTERLEDGER, . . .)

Taking the idea of IOTA or the hashgraph to the next level, one could combine the advantages of a blockchain (coin supply, general consensus, account creation) with that of scaling through a peer-to-peer network. For example, the **Lightning Network** that is focused on Bitcoin, the **Raiden Network** that is focused on Ethereum, or the **Interledger Protocol** that is focused on banking.

The future of blockchain technologies will be these blockchain-connecting technologies, as they provide stability and scalability at the same time.

GEEKY
Payment Channels
Instead of sending each other coins via informing everyone on the blockchain, they put the coins into the payment channel, which acts as a smart contract—no one can take

the coins back out unless they had the prior agreement of the other before. Sending someone coins would basically mean getting the agreement that I could take the coins out. Next, you can connect such payment channels from different blockchains, thereby forming so-called Atomic Swaps.

Atomic Swaps

Atomic swaps connect different payments channels, for example Ethereum and Bitcoin. If I send you bitcoin in one channel, you automatically give me Ether in the other. Imagine it like you having bitcoin in your left hand, and me having Ether in my right hand. If you give me your bitcoin, I have to give you my Ether, but if you keep your bitcoin, I automatically keep my Ether. It is a trustless swap. With this, one can then put such channels after each other via so-called HTLCs (Hashed Time Lock Contracts).

HTLCs (Hashed Time Lock Contracts)

HTLCs put Atomic Swaps in a chain after each other and work like this: I give you bitcoin that you give to your friend, who then gives you Ether that you give to me. All happening instantly and completely secure, as no one can abort due to cryptographic reasons. You can then connect other people though such a system. Since you and I can do an unlimited amount of transactions, there is no scalability challenge, while the underlying blockchains provide the basic infrastructure for such a system to actually work.

GEEKY OFF

CHAPTER 11 – CRYPTO-INVESTING

Knowing everything you know by now, you might already be excited to invest in these new applications. Maybe you feel the opposite, and you see way more dangers than opportunities. Both feelings are understandable, but only one will be right. Since you have all this knowledge now, it might be a good idea to get onto the side that is.

SHOULD YOU INVEST INTO CRYPTOCURRENCIES?

Instead of me telling you my opinion, which you can guess anyways, let me tell you about the World Economic Forum's prediction that all cryptocurrencies combined will reach around 7-8 trillion USD by 2025. The total market cap right now is not even at 4% of that in 2017. In my opinion Bitcoin alone could achieve that. So, there is a huge growth-, BUT also big risk potential! Remember, most of the cryptocurrencies have not yet stood the test of time, and none of them have been around for longer than a decade. Compare it to the 1990s: if you could have invested into "the internet," you would have become rich. But, you had to pick actual applications, since "the internet" is not really a thing to invest in. Over 99% of these applications went bankrupt during the dot-com bubble. Could I invest "into blockchain," I would invest everything I own. But just like in the internet example, this is not possible. One has to select the applications, or in the case of blockchain technologies, the cryptocurrencies. Here I am also expecting that most of these cryptocurrencies will go to 0, while a few will prevail and become worth billions and trillions.

ARE CRYPTOCURRENCIES IN A BUBBLE?

I hope so! Not the answer you expected, right? Let me explain: bubbles are some of the most important features of the economic machine. They are absolutely essential, as they give easy capital to companies that want to grow during the bubble phase, but then weed out the weak companies when the bubble bursts. The trick as a company is to be strong and cash-rich, with a great team and lots of customers. As an investor, the trick is to spread your risks while not becoming greedy. This starts with the following important question:

WHAT IS THE RISK-REWARD-RATIO OF INVESTING INTO CRYPTOCURRENCIES?

In investing, one of the most important questions you can ask yourself is what is the potential down- and what is the potential upside? Afterwards, ask yourself what is the likelihood of either scenario happening? Let's use real estate as an example. It is the beginning of 2018. Where could real estate drop to, and what could it go up to? This highly depends on the area you live in of course, but if we use a place like Las Vegas, we could imagine that if a bad crash happens, it could drop 50%. In a best case, it could go up another 10%, but probably not more, since we are quite high already. What is the likelihood of either? A 50% drop happens every 10 years or so, so it is around a 10% chance per year. For it to go up 10% is probably a 25% chance. Everything else is somewhere in the middle. So, what does this mean for investing? Just looking at the numbers, it surprises me how many people are looking into real estate at the moment because the numbers look horrific in my opinion. There is quite a chance your money halves, and there is not that big of a chance that it goes up. So why take the risk? If you want a formula for it, you could say:

10 % upside x 20 % probability = 2 % up

25 % downside x 10 % probability = 2,5 % down

So, if you had an unlimited amount of opportunities and real estate was a "perfect market" right now, you would actually end up losing money if you invested at current prices, since you would go 2.5 steps forward and 5 steps backwards repeatedly. Obviously, this is highly theoretical and just serves demonstrative purposes. We could do this for stocks, real estate, currencies, bonds, etc., and it will tell you why smart investors are not investing much into these asset classes at the moment. Now, let's do the same calculations for cryptocurrencies.

The world economic forum predicts the aforementioned 25x upside, but let's just use 10x for this calculation. This might happen with a 20% probability. In cryptocurrencies, you can definitely lose everything, so you have 100% downside, with a probability of 10%. The reason I choose less than 20% is that I personally think it is more likely for cryptocurrencies as a whole to be successful, rather than them going to 0. This assumes not betting on one individual currency, but on an entire group to diversify the risk. You might want to plug in your own numbers, but let's look at these calculations of mine:

1.000 % upside with a 20 % probability = 200 % up
100 % downside with a10 % probability = 10 % down

Looking at numbers of cryptocurrencies one thing becomes very clear:

YOU CAN DEFINITELY LOSE ALL YOUR MONEY!

However, while going 200 steps forward, on average you only go

10 steps backwards in the example we used. There is NO guarantee that this will be the likely scenario, it is just some of my own thinking of why I invest in cryptocurrencies:

The risk / reward ratio is very attractive!

Ask any professional poker player. "No one knows what the future will bring, but I do like to have my probabilities right!" - And I love doing the same in investing.

HOW MUCH SHOULD YOU INVEST INTO CRYPTO?

Before you run off to invest all your money, here is a reminder once again:

You can lose all your money. Therefore, do NOT invest more than you are willing to lose!

I personally would recommend you investing at least a little bit into cryptocurrencies. If you are completely scared, try 50 USD. If you are a calculated risk taker, do around 5-10% of your liquid capital. If you are more cautious, do less. The upside is huge, but be aware that you might lose it all. Obviously, the larger the market capitalization of a cryptocurrency, such as Bitcoin or Ethereum has, the lesser the risk.

WHEN IS THE BEST TIME TO INVEST?

"The best time was yesterday; the second-best time is today."

While this quote is definitely not always right, it highlights something: The earlier you get into a growing market, the better. However, since you might always fall into the trap of hitting a peak, my personal strategy is to split money into three parts. Assume you want to invest 900 USD, then it would be 3x 300. Invest the first 300 USD immediately and diversify it among some of the larger coins. Once the market dips, and it always will, invest the 2nd part. Wait, and once the market dips again, do the third part. That way you have a very nice average-effect over time. If you have extra cash along the way, you can always buy more of certain coins.

WHAT IS THE BEST CRYPTO INVESTING STRATEGY?

NO ONE knows which cryptocurrency will go up or which one will go down, and anyone who tells you he knows for sure is a liar. No one knows. Sadly, there are too many of these charlatans out there, and people fall for their hype. If you want to be a successful cryptocurrency investor, stay away from these people and focus on these proven success strategies:

1. Diversify over time: Do not invest it all at one go.
2. Diversify over currencies: For example, I have 10-15 different cryptocurrencies at the moment.
3. Do NOT trust hypes or dumps in the media or from influencers. They usually do NOT know the market better than anyone else.
4. If you had always wanted to buy a coin and it drops, buy it. It

makes no sense not to buy a coin, just because it dropped. Actually, the opposite is true, as you should buy more now since it has just become cheaper.

5. Warren Buffett teaches: "If you want to make a lot of money investing, buy low and sell high!" It is really simple, and the reason most people don't do that is because they get distracted and follow the masses.

6. Do NOT look for getting rich quick schemes. If you are promised high returns, stay away. No one can promise high returns.

7. You probably have heard of COMPOUNDING, which Albert Einstein called the 8th wonder of the world. For example, if you double your money every year (100% per year), you have 1-thousand-folded it over 10 years! 1,000 USD would bring you 1 Million USD! ($2^{\wedge}10 = 1024$). So, be patient.

8. If you want to sell a coin, never sell it all. Always keep a very small amount. You never know what happens, and maybe this part goes 100x. I had this with Ripple in early 2017, where I made 40x with a small part that I had kept for quite some time after selling the rest.

9. Get around other successful cryptocurrency investors. Either join a Mastermind group, or go to events and meetups. If you are reading this and you want me to speak at your event, contact us via team@julianhosp.com - I would be happy to do so.

10. Do not day trade—HODL, and that is not a typo.

WHAT IS "HODL?"

HODL means "to hold" and comes from a famous Bitcointalk entry, where one angry drunk user complained about his girl leaving him, him losing all his money in Bitcoin, and him just giving a s**t about this, as he will simply "HODL." What he meant was that he wanted to keep holding bitcoins until they go back up and not caring about the dip. The typo stuck, and today millions of people in the crypto-ecosystem talk about HODL when they mean "hold" by not selling.

HOW TO MEASURE PROFITS PROPERLY

Whenever you invest in something and make a profit, you have to measure the returns against something else to know whether it made sense or not. If, for example, you invest into a highly risky cryptocurrency, and you make 20% profit per year, it may sound great at first. If, on the other hand, Bitcoin makes 30% gains during the same time, you actually lose 10%, because Bitcoin, being the largest and most respected cryptocurrency, is traditionally seen as the investment with the lowest risk in that field. Low risk in that regard still means high risk in general, of course. One thing I personally started to do is to measure my entire portfolio against a 50/50 split of Bitcoin and Ethereum, to see if what I am doing actually makes sense and whether I am making a profit, or whether it would have just made better sense to stay in Bitcoin and Ethereum altogether. In 2017, for example, I had a friend who told me how proud he was that with all his trading and investing into over 100 different currencies, he had tripled his money. That is very impressive, however, had he just stayed in a 50/50 split of BTC and ETH, he would have had gains from around 1,000 USD in January 2017 to over 8,000 USD at the end of 2017 in Bitcoin, and from 10 USD to over 400 USD in Ethereum. That is a 24x return with no work and the risk of being in the largest and most respected cryptocurrencies of that year. The point being: Do not only use USD as a measuring stick, but rather pick an "index" within the industry.

WHICH CRYPTOCURRENCIES TO PICK

No one knows which cryptocurrencies will be the winners, so it is best if you create a diversified portfolio of these currencies that you bet on. If you don't want to make selections yourself, there are more and more companies trying to create something like a fund, where you just have to invest into one thing and automatically invest into an array of currencies. Melonport is an example of that. I mostly focus on cryptocurrencies that have a strong economic advantage over others, a strong community, great developers, and a convincing vision for what they want to achieve. I hardly jump on "a new trend" or go for a hype coin, as pump and dumps are not what I am interested in. Search for "Julian Hosp circle schemes" if you want to read a blog post I wrote on that.

WINTER IS COMING!

My belief is that most of the coins will probably go to 0 over time, and with that I mean over 99% of them. However, the 1% will not only make up for all the losses, but can actually make you rich. Many times, we have a rising tide, and it appears as if all ideas and coins will be successful. This is not because of the idea itself but because of the entire ecosystem going up. People get lured into investing into any coin, even so-called sh*t-coins. However, remember this: As long as the tide is high, you don't know who is swimming naked. As soon as the water recedes, the truth comes out. Crypto winter will come at some point.

No one knows when and how, so the only thing you can do is to be prepared and don't fall for shiny objects that actually do not deliver any real value. One of the reasons I do have a mastermind group around this topic and why I do speak at so many events is to stay up-to-date and not fall for prejudice myself, but rather, get radical feedback on investment ideas. I can recommend you to do the same.

HOW TO GET YOUR FIRST CRYPTOCURRENCIES

If you decide to get your first cryptocurrencies, you have two options:

1. If you plan on investing a million USD or more, use a so-called over-the-counter service (OTC), where you can buy cryptocurrencies directly without going through an exchange. Contact, for example, www.kraken.com for more info. I am NOT affiliated with them, but I have used their services successfully in the past. There are several others, and you will find many on Google. Be careful NOT to fall for scams, so do your due diligence. With OTC, you basically transfer them fiat (USD, EUR, …), and they send you the cryptocurrencies you want from someone, who is selling them that very moment. Minimum amounts are typically 1 million USD or more.

2. If you don't intend on investing a million USD, yet ;-), then you should register on an exchange. These are services where you can use your credit card or bank account to buy cryptocurrencies with USD, EUR, or other fiat currencies. Mostly, you can only buy bitcoins or Ether with fiat, and then you need to use those to buy other cryptocurrencies. When registering on an exchange, you will have to do KYC (Know Your Customer) by uploading your passport and proof of address. Every legit exchange will request

that from you. These are the exchanges I am using myself. I am NOT endorsing them, just sharing my own experience:

- www.kraken.com (great for bank transfers and offer several currencies)
- www.coinbase.com (great for credit card purchases)
- https://www.bitcoin.de/de/r/pkapgd (great for German users with Fidor accounts)
- www.bittrex.com (offers a lot of different cryptocurrencies)

Even if you don't intend to invest straight away, you should get an account with one or more of them, as verification times sometimes take several weeks due to the large demand. The steps that follow are simple:

1. Register
2. Get verified
3. Transfer fiat
4. Get cryptocurrencies
5. Store cryptocurrencies safely

WHAT HAPPENED WITH MTGOX?

The step of storing cryptocurrencies safely is crucial. If you still remember the chapter about wallets, you will remember that one of the most important things in cryptocurrencies is to control your own private key. Exchanges do not let you do that, so if an exchange has a problem or a fork happens, you are at the exchange's mercy. One of the worst examples in history was the collapse of the exchange MtGox in

2013, where a lot of people lost access to their coins. The solution is to move your cryptocurrencies OFF an exchange as soon as you buy them and you don't intend on selling them right away. You can search for "Julian Hosp bitcoin VIP webinar," where I go into a lot of detail on the mechanics, if you want.

WHERE TO KEEP YOUR CRYPTOCURRENCIES

I have talked about how to store your cryptocurrencies in great detail in the wallet chapter. In case you can't remember it that well anymore, jump back there, as I will build on top of that knowledge.

I keep my cryptocurrencies in the following way:

- I use exchanges only briefly to buy or trade. I only keep cryptocurrencies on there if there are no good wallets for a certain coin or it is such a small amount that setting everything up is more work than the risk of leaving it on the exchange.
- I keep a bit of Bitcoin and Ether in a wallet as a HOT storage so I can spend them anytime if I have to. I treat this wallet like I would treat any wallet with USD inside, and I am aware that I could lose this money, but it would not be the end of the world. Additionally, I use the Bread Wallet www.breadwallet. com for Bitcoin and www.myetherwallet.com for Ethereum and ERC20 tokens. I also use the Jaxx wallet for some other coins: www.jaxx.io.
- Most of my coins are in a cold-storage on my hard wallet: www.julianhosp.com/hardwallet.

I have written down the private key for my cold storage on three pieces of paper, and I am storing these keys in different safety deposit boxes. Such a system is relatively cheap (around 100 USD for the hard-wallet and around 40 USD a year for the safety deposit boxes) but insanely safe. It is very difficult to ever lose access to the private keys, and the risk of getting hacked is very low. You need to put the danger of natural disasters, fires and water damage into account. If you are just starting out with a few dollars, then leaving everything on an exchange is absolutely ok, as long as it is not too much money. You should learn to have your own wallets, even if they are "HOT" as soft wallets at the beginning. Once the invested amounts get bigger, you should invest into a hard-wallet and have a proper key management system.

One big business opportunity for the future will be a simple, yet safe, solution on how to store one's private keys, but also how to will them as an inheritance. This will be a key requirement for cryptocurrencies to truly achieve mass adoption.

WHEN SHOULD YOU SELL A CRYPTOCURRENCY?

Answering this question is just as tough as when to buy. Generally speaking, I sell a coin when it has gone up way more than others. I hardly ever sell for dollars but mostly for other coins that might have underperformed and have promising technologies. I never sell a coin completely, as you never know if it pops at a later stage. I never try to predict the market, but I rather adapt to what has happened: If a coin goes up a lot, I rebalance by selling parts of it. If it dips, I purchase more with either dollars or the profits from other coins. I believe there will come a time in 7-10 years where the question will not be centered around when should you sell your coins anymore because cryptocurrencies will not be measured in dollars anymore. They will just be another accepted currency, and they will be worth a lot, in my opinion. So,

I buy them cheap, while I still can.

HOW ARE CRYPTOCURRENCIES TAXED?

Taxation is different from country to country, and I can highly recommend you consulting a tax expert in your area to give you a clear answer. One thing I urge is that you do NOT try to avoid taxes through cryptocurrencies. They are less private than you think, and doing some shady things in this department will get you big time. So, you better be a law-abiding citizen and stick to the rules. One important thing I feel regulators should look into is to differentiate between taxes from speculating vs. spending cryptocurrencies. Some countries such as Australia are doing that already and I hope many others will follow. That brings us to the next question:

HOW TO SPEND CRYPTOCURRENCIES?

Looking at the key requirements of a currency as being a unit of account, store of value, and method of transfer, one can see that a currency is not only there to be stored, but to be spent (unit of account and method of transfer). That is one of the biggest challenges cryptocurrencies are facing right now: They are not really spendable—yet. The ideal scenario would be that customers and businesses would both agree on a cryptocurrency and use that to interact. That future will come, but it will still take a bit.

Until then, several companies are trying to bridge the gap until that moment. BitPay, for example, offers a service to merchants where they can accept cryptocurrencies, but the business actually receives dollars or euros. The cryptocurrency price automatically adjusts via the exchange rate to the underlying cryptocurrency, which makes it risk-free for the merchant and attractive for customers who want to make a purchase while using cryptocurrencies.

CHAPTER 12 – THE FUTURE OF CRYPTOCURRENCIES

So, what can the future of cryptocurrencies look like?

WHAT WILL PAYMENTS LOOK LIKE IN 5-7 YEARS?

Aside from more points of acceptance and better usability, we will see tokenization of pretty much any asset over the next 5-7 years. This means that things like stocks, real estate, gold, and literally any other thing will get a token that is represented in a blockchain. This will lead to seamless communication between these assets and to better price discovery.

WHAT IS PRICE DISCOVERY?

Price discovery allows for better pricing of goods and services, as more people have access to them when markets become more liquid.

WHAT WILL PAYMENTS LOOK LIKE IN 10 YEARS?

If you believe that blockchains will be the only game in town, in my opinion, you will be wrong. There will always be a need for centralized institutions, but decentralized communities will challenge them to be at their best, so they cannot do whatever they want.

This will be the equilibrium that we will see setting in over the next 10 years.

WHAT WILL PAYMENTS LOOK LIKE IN 15–20 YEARS?

In 15-20 years, I envision that when you go somewhere to pay, your neurolinked brain communicates with assets on the blockchains. Through machine learning, the app chooses which assets to pay with and which ones to keep. It will be entirely seamless, without any friction, instant, safe, and at literally no cost all over the world, and maybe on other planets too. I know much of this sounds crazy right now, but this is what we thought about technology thirty years ago as well. Who would have thought that internet video calling is pretty much free today? The same will be true for cryptocurrencies, and you, by having read this book all the way to this point, have laid the foundation to be prepared for the decentralized revolution.

The first step into a new topic is always the scariest one. I not only want to thank you for your trust to having taken this step together with me, but furthermore want to congratulate you for going on this journey. Many more exciting things lie ahead of you.

BONUS CHAPTER: INITIAL COIN OFFERINGS (ICO)

The topic of ICOs was covered briefly in chapter 10, however, I wanted to throw in a bonus chapter about what they are, why they are relevant, and how you can benefit from them both as a company and as a potential investor. In this bonus chapter, I want to share some of the lessons learned doing an ICO.

WHAT IS AN ICO?

An ICO or Initial Coin Offering is a way for a company or organization to create their own cryptocurrency and then offer it to others publicly for purchase.

This cryptocurrency can have their own blockchain, such as Ethereum did in 2014, or it can be token-based on top of another platform, such as the ERC20 tokens based on Ethereum. The latter is actually the most common route. In an ICO, the buyers of a company's token exchanges cryptocurrencies with the company in return for the newly created token. The company receives the money, the buyer the token.

HOW IS AN ICO DIFFERENT THAN AN IPO?

An IPO, or Initial Public Offering, is the event of a company offering their shares to the public. The company receives the investors' money, the investor receives shares and owns part of the company. An IPO requires an investor prospectus, as the investors who now own part of the company have clear rights and insights. An ICO is very different, in that a proper ICO offers a new cryptocurrency that, per-se, does not offer much of any rights. Normally, a token does NOT offer any ownership in the company and should be seen as in independent "thing" that may or may not increase in value. It is more of a "hope of the token buyer" that the company will do with the money what they proposed to do. This is very different than an actual security, even though many tokens come close. As an investor, it also means that you must understand that an ICO has incomparably higher risks than an IPO.

WHAT IS A TOKEN SALE / TOKEN GENERATING EVENT?

You might have heard that companies call an ICO a token sale or token generating event. While some of the legalities behind them might be different, the process for a token buyer is quite similar. You can call your event a token sale and make it similar to a Kickstarter campaign, where a company sells for example 10,000 backpacks for 100 USD each, receiving 1 million USD in total. After the sale is done, the company has no more duties other than to fulfill the function of the token.

WHY DO COMPANIES DO ICOS?

Generally speaking, a company needs a few things to launch: a good idea, even better execution, and a rock star team to do all that. With that comes the challenge of financing the entire operation. While traditional methods of financing through Angels or VCs are possible, the crypto world has turned towards this new form of direct business to investor financing called ICOs. The upside for the company is that they can receive a lot more money without giving up any equity (piece of their company) if they do a good job. The upside for the token buyer is that an ICO can be very attractive as an investment.

WHAT MAKES A SUCCESSFUL ICO?

The big problem that remains is that most companies doing an ICO are still startups. Pure statistics tell that 99% of all startups fail—therefore, also ICOs. If you, as a company, want to do a successful ICO or you want to find ICOs that are more likely to succeed as an investor, look out for these five key points:

1. Have a great and compelling **IDEA** that solves a real-world problem.
2. Have an even better **EXECUTION**, as ideas are worth very little if not acted upon.
3. Have a kickass **TEAM** with developers, product people, legal, structure, marketing, and much more.
4. Make sure the **TOKEN's** legal obligations and the ICO's financials are sound. What are the market cap, price, structure, token function, etc.?

5. Look for excellent **COMMUNICATION**. If a team is not

transparent or reachable, step away.

SHOULD YOU INVEST IN ICOS?

That is entirely up to you. If you do great due diligence and you are aware that most ICOs will fail, you can dip your toe into this water. You can participate in these ICOs through the companies' websites or buy the tokens afterwards. Be aware of the risks when participating in startups, and make sure you compare your returns to the right "index", for example the afore mentioned 50/50 split of Bitcoin and Ethereum. If your risky token beats that mix by far, which very very few tokens have ever done, then it is worth the investment. You can find an overview of ongoing ICOs here: https://www.smithandcrown.com/icos/

WHERE CAN YOU FIND MORE INFO ON ICOS?

I wanted to post this brief bonus chapter, as I know ICOs are a very hot topic right now. If you want to read a whole lot more about it, search for my latest content: "Julian Hosp Initial Coin Offerings ICOs." Have fun investing in ICOs, and remember to stay safe.

WHAT'S NEXT?

Congrats, you've made it! Now, you have a very solid insight into blockchain, cryptocurrencies, and how they will affect our lives.

Are you wondering what your first steps should look like in order to become even more #CRYPTOFIT?

Let me give you a few TO DOs right now:

1. **Download the checklist** with some tips and tricks here, if you haven't done so already: www.cryptofit.community/workbook Work through the questions and summary.

2. Remember that many things in the crypto ecosystem are moving fast. Some links, exchanges, or currencies might not exist any longer by the time you read this. Go to events. If you are an event organizer and you want me to speak, contact our team at team@julianhosp.com

3. Join us on **Facebook** and interact with others: www.facebook.com/groups/cryptofit. Surround yourself with people who stay on top of things, just like you do. **Google "Julian Hosp Crypto Mastermind Group"** if you want to join our community, or create one yourself.

4. One last thing: if you got value out of this book, then **help me on my vision** to make people all around the world become #CRYTPOTFIT. Share this book with a few loved ones. Give it to them as a present. Post a link on Facebook or Twitter. Most of all, leave me a review on Amazon. Simply go to www.amazon.com, search for Julian Hosp Cryptocurrencies, and drop

me some feedback. It would mean the world to me and would spread the word and help to make others cryptofit.

Be open about blockchain and cryptocurrencies. Try it out. See it like the internet 30 years ago: Those who moved first were the winners, and those who kept betting on offline lost. Be smart, stay agile, and keep learning. Remember, knowledge is only potential power. Execution trumps knowledge all day long. So, since you finished this book, go and take action!

When people ask me what my purpose in life is, I answer: "It is to create options, not only for myself, but also for others." I love to have options as I believe this is what lets me be more successful. That is why I want to make people #CRYPTOFIT, as this is what brings people options. They can then decide to stay in a centralized world if they want to, but they have the option to change anytime. That is what is truly liberating: knowing you can. With this, I want to thank you. I wish you all the best and hope to see you someday, somewhere in person—or maybe hear from you in an email.

Keep being awesome, stay #CRYPTOFIT, and rock this world.

Yours truly
Julian Hosp

ABOUT THE AUTHOR

 Dr. Julian Hosp, born in 1986, is a professional athlete, medical doctor, entrepreneur, cryptocurrency expert, and bestselling author.

Julian pursued his studies in Innsbruck, as well as at a high school in Nashville, Tennessee, in the United States. Afterwards, he became a professional kite surfer for almost 10 years, where he was ranked among the Top 10 in the world. He was a trauma surgeon before leaving that career in pursuit of his entrepreneurial desires. In 2013, Julian published the bestselling kitesurfing book called Kite-Tricktionary, and in 2015, he released 25 Stories I would tell my Younger Self.

Today, Julian is a serial entrepreneur, bestselling author, and keynote-speaker. He has also been named one of the top blockchain and cryptocurrency experts in the world. Furthermore, he is a frequently invited speaker at global Tech/Fintech events, as well as a regular commentator in the media on current blockchain trends, the future of cryptocurrency, and best practices. Also he advises groups of the European Parliament on blockchain and ICO's.

Being based in Singapore, but travelling most of the time for his business ventures, Julian pursues his passion for cryptocurrencies, sports, and public speaking, all while maintaining his laser-focus drive. For the most recent info, follow him on any social media and get connected.

FURTHER READING

BLOCKCHAIN 2.0: FAR MORE THAN JUST BITCOIN

https://geni.us/blockchain_simple

What would happen, if your data could be saved in a way absolutely secure and not hackable?

Right now Bitcoin and cryptocurrency is on everyone's lips, but the term ‚blockchain' is hiding so much more. Data protection, tokenization, the smart contract and ownership are just a few of a high number of applications possible.

This book contains everything about the possibilities, the potential and the dangers of decentralized applications. After his bestseller „Cryptocurrencies - Bitcoin, Ethereum, Blockchain, ICO's & Co. simply explained", now Dr. Julian Hosp is committed to explaining the blockchain in a simple way. Therefore, this book is suitable for everyone who wants to prepared for the coming world of blockchain.

25 STORIES I WOULD TELL MY YOUNGER SELF

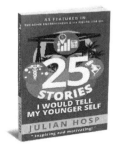

https://geni.us/25stories

„This book motivates anyone to find their purpose in life!"
Are you feeling a bit lost and looking for new inspiration?
Have you always wanted to find true motivation in your life?
Do you love reading exciting real experiences of successful people?
In this book bestselling author Dr. Julian Hosp tells
25 encouraging, but also shocking stories from his life, how he
found answers to all these questions and which 75 essential
lessons he would give to a younger self today, to reach the goal
of financial freedom much faster.
He talks about dazzling parties and all the experiences of ten years
of professional kitesurfing around the world and what that means
to him today. He takes the reader into the decision as to why he studied medicine, but did not work as a doctor and whether he regrets
that in retrospect. He describes his first businesses in his childhood
and how they made it possible for him to become a serial entrepreneur today. And he breaks down the details of how he became a
millionaire out of debt in just a few years and how he would make
it even faster today.

https://geni.us/timehorizon_en

How do the most successful people in the world manage to create work-life balance? How do they seem to effortlessly achieve all the great business, money, family or health benefits? How do these people put their daily 24 hours to use?

Spiegel bestselling author Dr. Julian Hosp brings light into the darkness by asking questions and answers from his Timehorizon mentor, who has worked with many of these successful people. Like a secret elixir, Julian applies it in his business and increases the value of his company by several hundred million dollars within a few years. His professional network now extends to the most successful people in the world and his relationship with his wife Bettina and his family is more loving than ever. He runs a marathon, is fitter than ever, learns Chinese and programming. With Timehorizon everything suddenly becomes quite simple.

In this masterpiece, the reader plunges into a world of productivity that he has never experienced before. If you have always wondered how you should divide up the hours of the day for your income, your family, and yourself to get the most out of it, you will be loving this book as tens of thousands of other people have before.

CONTENT

Mission
Mixers
Money
Mtgox

N
Namecoin (nmc)
Network
Node
Non-blockchain coins
Nonce

O
Open source
Orphan blocks
Other "decentralized platforms"
Over-the-counter services (otc)

P
Paper money
Paper-wallet
Passive income
Physical money
Pre-mined
Price discovery
Price prediction
Privacy
Private coins
Private key
Proof of importance
Proof of stake

Proof of work
Pseudo anonymity
Public address
Purchase done with bitcoins

Q
Quantum computing

R
Rai stones
Regulation
Replay attacks
Ring signatures

S
Satoshi nakamoto
Scaling debate
Scaling solutions
Scam
Scams
Secrecy
Seed
Segwit
Simple payment verification (spv)
Smart contracts
Soft-wallet
Splits
Staking
Storage
Strands
Sybil attack

Printed in Great Britain
by Amazon